THE ASSASSINATION OF JOHN F. KENNEDY

BY SUE BRADFORD EDWARDS

CONTENT CONSULTANT

HARVEY KLEHR
PROFESSOR EMERITUS, POLITICAL SCIENCE
EMORY UNIVERSITY

AMERICAN CRIME STORIES

An Imprint of Abdo Publishing | abdobooks.com

ABDOBOOKS.COM

Published by Abdo Publishing, a division of ABDO, PO Box 398166, Minneapolis, Minnesota 55439.

Printed in the United States of America, North Mankato, Minnesota.
102019
012020

Cover Photos: AP Images, left; Jim Altgens/AP Images, right
Interior Photos: AP Images, 4–5, 13, 20, 22, 24, 92; James W. Ike Altgens/AP Images, 10–11; National Archives - JFK/Corbis Historical/Getty Images, 17, 28, 31, 33, 69; Schulman-Sachs/picture-alliance/dpa/AP Images, 37; Lee Corkran/Sygma/Getty Images, 40–41; Cecil Stoughton/The White House/AP Images, 43; Corbis Historical/Getty Images, 47; Cecil Stoughton/PhotoQuest/Getty Images, 50; Brendan Smialowski/AFP/Getty Images, 54–55; Teresa Otto/Shutterstock Images, 60; James K.W. Atherton/The Washington Post/Getty Images, 65; LM Otero/AP Images, 75; AugustSnow/Alamy, 80–81; Gary S. Settles/Science Source, 84; Ian Halperin/UPI/Alamy, 87; Red Line Editorial, 89; Susan Walsh/AP Images, 97

Editor: Charly Haley
Series Designer: Melissa Martin

LIBRARY OF CONGRESS CONTROL NUMBER: 2019941918

PUBLISHER'S CATALOGING-IN-PUBLICATION DATA

Names: Edwards, Sue Bradford, author.
Title: The assassination of John F. Kennedy / by Sue Bradford Edwards
Description: Minneapolis, Minnesota: Abdo Publishing, 2020 | Series: American crime stories | Includes online resources and index.
Identifiers: ISBN 9781532190087 (lib. bdg) | ISBN 9781532175930 (ebook)
Subjects: LCSH: Kennedy, John F. (John Fitzgerald), 1917-1963--Juvenile literature. | Presidents--Assassination--United States--Juvenile literature. | Political murder--Juvenile literature. | Politics and government--Juvenile literature.
Classification: DDC 973.922--dc23

CONTENTS

CHAPTER ONE

THE ASSASSINATION

On November 22, 1963, President John F. Kennedy arrived in Dallas, Texas. He had not publicly announced that he was going to run for reelection in 1964, but those close to him knew his plans. Kennedy was a very popular president among Americans and around the world. In September, to start gathering support for his campaign, he had launched a series of trips, speaking in various parts of the United States. On this particular trip, a two-day, five-city Texas tour, he was accompanied by his wife, Jacqueline Kennedy.

President John F. Kennedy, *left*, and his wife, Jackie, arrive in Dallas on November 22, 1963.

PRESS TELEPHONES
TELEP

There was light rain that day, but by the time Kennedy's motorcade headed through Dallas, the weather had cleared. In rainy weather, the president's limousine convertible was fitted with a plastic bubble, a shield against weather that still allowed voters to see him. Because the rain had stopped, a Secret Service agent had removed the bubble top. A pair of agents rode in the front seat, one of them driving the car. Behind them, sitting in a second row of seats, was Texas governor John Connally and his wife, Nellie Connally. The Kennedys sat in the back seat.

For further protection, special running boards had been installed on the sides and back of the limousine to allow Secret Service agents to ride standing on the outside of the car. These running boards kept the agents close to the Kennedys in case

WHY DALLAS? WHY THEN?

Kennedy wanted to be in Dallas on November 22, 1963, because that's when the Dallas Citizens Council was sponsoring a lunch meeting at the Trade Mart. To win reelection as president, Kennedy, a Democrat, believed he needed the support of the Texas Democratic Party because Texas was overwhelmingly Democrat at the time. But the Texas Democratic Party was divided because of arguments between liberal Democrats and conservative Democrats. Kennedy needed a united party behind him. The hope was that if leaders of the Citizens Council, who were among the most influential people in Dallas politics, heard a rousing speech by the president, they would work to smooth out the differences within the party and help carry Kennedy to victory in the next election.

of an emergency, but they were not used during the president's Dallas visit. Kennedy reportedly thought being surrounded by agents made him look less friendly and too distant from the people.

The Secret Service code name for Kennedy's limousine was X-100.

However, for more protection, Secret Service agents followed Kennedy's limousine in a second car. The agents both rode in this car and stood on its running boards. Behind this second car, several more cars carried Vice President Lyndon B. Johnson and his wife, Claudia "Lady Bird" Johnson, White House staff, Texas politicians and staff, and reporters. Leading the motorcade were police motorcycles and a car carrying Jesse Curry, the Dallas chief of police. The motorcade traveled a ten-mile (16 km) route through downtown Dallas, ending at the Trade Mart, where Kennedy was scheduled to speak at the Dallas Citizens Council, a gathering of influential business leaders.

Because a target moving fast is harder to hit than a target moving slowly, a presidential motorcade usually drives up to twice the posted speed limit. But Kennedy wanted to be seen by the people of Dallas. Where there were no people lining the street, the motorcade drove at 25 to 30 mph (40 to 48 kmh), but where there were crowds, it slowed to just 11 mph (18 kmh) as Kennedy waved to the people lining the streets.[1] This slow

THE CAR'S BUBBLE TOP

The plastic bubble top made to fit the presidential convertible was a safety measure, but not in the way many people may assume. If a bullet was fired at the right angle to the shield, it might ricochet and be deflected away from its human target, but the plastic shield was neither bullet-resistant nor bulletproof. There was no guarantee it would stop a bullet. However, experts say using the bubble top would have protected Kennedy by simply obscuring the president, making him a more difficult target for a shooter.

speed worried the Secret Service agents because people could interfere with the vehicle or attack it. This would be more difficult to do if the car's protective bubble top had been in place, but it was not used. In addition to driving at a slow speed, the motorcade made several unscheduled stops for Kennedy to interact with groups of people along the way.

Around 12:30, the motorcade left Main Street and turned into Dealey Plaza. As in other parts of the city, cheering crowds lined the street, and the Kennedys waved to them. Jackie Kennedy would later recall looking ahead to where the street passed through a tunnel under the highway: "I remember thinking it would be so cool under that tunnel."[2]

Then a gunshot rang out. A bullet hit President Kennedy in his neck. In the middle seat, Governor Connally had also been hit.

Secret Service agent Clint Hill was riding on one of the running boards of the second convertible. He heard an explosive sound. As he looked for what had caused the sound, he saw Kennedy lurch to the side and grab his neck. Despite the fact that he wasn't wearing a bulletproof vest, Hill knew he needed to shield the Kennedys, and that meant getting to them. He jumped off the running board and sprinted to the Kennedys' limousine.

As Hill pulled himself onto the back of the convertible, another shot was fired, striking Kennedy in his head. Agent Hill pushed the First Lady down to protect her from the gunfire. Then he laid his own body across the back seat of the car to shield the Kennedys. As Hill did this, the car accelerated, speeding toward Parkland Memorial Hospital.

UNSCHEDULED STOPS

Before the motorcade reached the turn into Dealey Plaza, it drove down Lemmon Avenue. There, Kennedy saw a group of children with a handmade sign that said, "Please Stop And Shake Our Hands."[3] When he saw the sign, Kennedy directed the agent driving the car to stop, despite the fact that the Secret Service disliked unexpected stops. They knew Kennedy wanted to connect with the American people, but to protect the president, the agents had to operate as if every such stop could be a trap. When the car stopped on Lemmon Avenue, Kennedy didn't get out, but he directed the children to come up to his car so he could shake their hands.

Secret Service agent Clint Hill pulls himself onto the back of President Kennedy's car shortly after the president was shot. First Lady Jackie Kennedy tries to help her wounded husband in the car.

At the Hospital

Dallas police radioed ahead to tell the hospital to expect a patient with a gunshot wound. The car topped 80 mph (129 kmh) as it raced to the hospital. As they sped to the hospital, Nellie Connally assured her injured husband that everything would be okay.

In the back seat, Kennedy's blood pooled on the floor of the car. Agent Hill lost his sunglasses as the wind swept over him, and he gripped the car, struggling not to fly off as they sped to the hospital. As the motorcade pulled up to the hospital, less than ten minutes after the third shot was fired, Secret Service agents with guns drawn surrounded the president's car to escort him inside.

But the First Lady refused to let go of her husband. Hill knew her well because he had often accompanied her when she traveled. He realized she didn't want people to see the president wounded. Hill removed his suit coat and used the garment to cover the president's upper body. Only then did Jackie Kennedy let the medical staff place her husband on a gurney and take him inside.

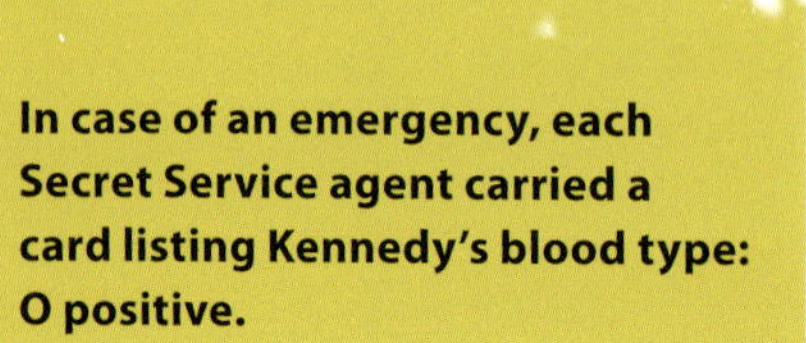

In case of an emergency, each Secret Service agent carried a card listing Kennedy's blood type: O positive.

Inside Trauma Room 1, doctors worked with Kennedy. They inserted a tracheotomy tube in his throat, hoping that an artificial airway would help him breathe. His heartbeat was uneven and weak. When his heartbeat stopped, a doctor tried to restart it by compressing Kennedy's chest—but this failed. There was nothing the doctors could do. At 1:00 p.m., they pronounced the president dead.

Police and other investigators had to move fast before the mysterious shooter could escape. Police talked to eyewitnesses who had been in Dealey Plaza, but people who had gathered to see the motorcade reported hearing and seeing different things. They couldn't agree on how many gunshots had been fired or what direction they had come from. But several people in and around the plaza had cameras to photograph

Daily Mail

NNEDY
SASSINATED

DAILY EXPRESS

KENNEDY
ASSASSINATED

A sniper's bullet

Daily Herald

Jackie cradles her husband after sniper blasts from window

ASSASSINATED!

Kennedy shot dead in car

Daily Mirror

KENNEDY
ASSASSINATED

Jackie spattered with blood

THE GUARDIAN

President Kenne

Shot beside wife in open car

DAILY SKETCH

GUNMAN HID ON FIFTH FLOOR—ATE FRIED CHICKEN AS HE WAITED

KENNEDY'S KILLER
—SUSPECT HELD

'Married to a Russian'

25 minutes to live

The Daily Telegraph

RESIDENT KENNEDY IS ASSASSINATE

ot in the head in open car on
exas festival drive

MRS. KENNEDY COMFORTS HE WOUNDED HUSBAND

S. KENNEDY SAFE:
VERNOR WOUNDED

NDON JOHNSON BECOMES
NEW PRESIDENT

WASHINGTON STUNNED BY NEWS OF SHOOTING

Newspapers all over the world reported Kennedy's death on their front pages.

and record the president's visit. One of these witnesses, dressmaker Abraham Zapruder, had filmed the whole thing. Thirty-one still shots of his film appeared in *Life* magazine on November 29, 1963.

News of the Assassination

At 1:38 p.m. on November 22, 1963, American broadcast journalist Walter Cronkite appeared on CBS television: "From Dallas, Texas, the flash, apparently official: President Kennedy died at 1:00 p.m., central standard time, 2:00 p.m., eastern standard time—some 38 minutes ago."[4]

TRAUMA ROOM 2

Texas governor John Connally was only semiconscious by the time the limousine reached Parkland Memorial Hospital. The Secret Service agents couldn't reach the president to get him out of the car with the governor still in the vehicle. Because of this, the agents first helped Connally out of the car and onto a gurney. The hospital staff took Connally to Trauma Room 2. Connally underwent four hours of surgery to repair injuries to his back, chest, wrist, and thigh. He had to wear a cast while his wrist healed, but Connally made a full recovery.

Many people were on their lunch breaks from work when the announcement was made. Restaurants and diners tuned television sets and radios to news stations. People gathered together to listen to the news. Reporters questioned people in the stunned crowds. When asked what she was feeling in the

LYNDON B. JOHNSON BECOMES PRESIDENT

Normally, a new president is sworn in at the Capitol Building in Washington, DC, by the chief justice of the Supreme Court. But when Kennedy was assassinated, Johnson was with him in Dallas. As vice president, Johnson became president as soon as Kennedy was declared dead. But he wasn't sworn in until 2:38 p.m., just over 90 minutes later. After the casket containing Kennedy's body was loaded onto Air Force One, Johnson, Lady Bird Johnson, Jackie Kennedy, and several Secret Service agents entered the plane, which would take them to Washington, DC. On the plane, Johnson was sworn in by Texas federal judge Sarah T. Hughes. Johnson put his hand not on a Bible, as per tradition, but on Kennedy's Catholic prayer book.

moment, one teen shook her head. "I really couldn't say. Right now, I just don't know what to do."[5] People entered churches and cathedrals, needing somewhere to grieve. But they also started to ask questions. Who did this? Who was behind the death of their president?

CHAPTER TWO

THE SHOOTER

When the assassin fired his first shot, it missed Kennedy entirely. The First Lady thought a police motorcycle had backfired. Others thought someone had set off a firecracker. Connally was a hunter and immediately recognized the sound as gunfire. Secret Service agent Paul Landis knew it was a gunshot, but he couldn't tell exactly where the shot had come from. He looked back toward the Texas School Book Depository Building and then scanned the crowd.

Witnesses confirmed the shot came from the Depository. One person saw a rifle barrel protruding out of an upper-story window on the building's southeast corner. Another witness saw the shooter clearly and provided investigators with a description. Inside the building, three employees had met on the fifth floor to watch the motorcade. They heard the shots fired from above, and one man had debris in his hair, shaken from the ceiling when the shots were fired. Another heard the

Dealey Plaza is the area of Dallas where Kennedy was shot. It also represents the place where the city of Dallas was founded in the 1840s.

Texas School Book Depository
Kennedy's car

EYEWITNESSES TO THE ASSASSINATION

About eight cars behind Kennedy's presidential limousine in Dallas was a press car carrying Robert H. Jackson, photographer for the *Dallas Times Herald*, and Malcolm Couch, a television news cameraman. Couch later told government investigators:

> *After the third shot, Bob Jackson, who was, as I recall, on my right, yelled something like, "Look up in the window! There's the rifle!" And I remember glancing up to a window on the far right, which at the time impressed me as the sixth or seventh floor, and seeing about a foot of a rifle being—the barrel brought into the window.*[1]

casings, ejected from the rifle, hit the floor. Police knew where to look for the shooter.

Finding the Assassin

After shooting Kennedy, the assassin hid his rifle and went down to the second floor of the Depository. By that time, Dallas police officer Marrion Baker and building superintendent Roy Truly were already climbing the stairs to reach the roof. They spotted a man in the second-floor lunchroom, but Truly recognized him as an employee of the Depository. Not suspecting the employee, Baker and Truly continued up to the roof. Meanwhile, that man, who was indeed the assassin, slipped outside. Only later would Baker realize the shooter could also be an employee of the Depository.

Just after 1:00 p.m., the assassin reached a boardinghouse where he had rented a room. He changed his jacket and put a pistol in his pocket. Then he left again on foot.

Back at the Depository, police searched the sixth floor. At approximately 1:12 p.m., a deputy found cartons arranged near the southeast window to form a sniper's nest. These boxes would help shelter the shooter from searching eyes. Near the window, the deputy found three spent rifle casings.

Based on witnesses' descriptions, police were searching for a white man, approximately 30 years old; 5 feet, 10 inches (1.8 m) tall; and weighing around 165 pounds (74.8 kg). At about 1:14 p.m., Officer J. D. Tippit of the Dallas police was patrolling the streets when he saw someone who fit this description. Tippit spoke to the man through the passenger window of his patrol car. After Tippit got out of the car to continue questioning the man, the man pulled a gun from his jacket pocket and killed Tippit.

Minutes later, at 1:22 p.m., two police officers at the Depository found a rifle between two stacks of boxes across the room from the sixth-floor window. Now police had the spent ammunition and the gun, but they still didn't know who had used them.

As police searched for the shooter, people across Dallas listened to the radio. Not far from the boardinghouse, Johnny Brewer, a shoe store manager, heard that both the president and a police officer had been shot. Moments later, a man stepped into the lobby of Brewer's store and waited as police

The Texas School Book Depository, *left*, has seven floors. Kennedy's assassin shot him from the sixth floor.

cars flew down the street, sirens wailing. After the sound of the sirens had grown faint, the man exited the building. Brewer was suspicious, so he followed the man to the Texas Theatre. Brewer waited there until the police arrived. Officers stopped the movie that had been playing in the theater. Once the lights had been turned on, Brewer went up on stage with two policemen and pointed out the suspicious man he had seen near his store.

By 1:50 p.m., the police had this man, Lee Harvey Oswald, in custody as a suspect in the shooting of Tippit.

Back at the Depository, police realized an employee would have easy access to the sixth floor. They had the managers take roll call. Only one employee was absent, though he had been present earlier in the day—Lee Harvey Oswald.

At 2:15 p.m., Dallas police captain J. W. Fritz returned to the police station from the Depository. He told officers to pick up Oswald because he may have shot Kennedy. "Captain, we will save you a trip," said Sergeant Gerald Hill. "Because there he sits."[2] Oswald was already in jail on suspicion of shooting Tippit. Now, he was being held in connection to the Kennedy assassination, too.

Oswald Shot

While the police held Oswald, the Federal Bureau of Investigation (FBI) traced the purchase of the rifle that had killed Kennedy to "A. Hidell."[3] When Oswald was arrested, the police had found two IDs in his wallet: one with the name Lee Harvey Oswald and another with the name Alek Hidell. Furthermore, the handwriting on the

The movie showing at the Texas Theatre when Lee Harvey Oswald took refuge there was a movie about World War II (1939–1945) called *War Is Hell*.

rifle's order form matched Oswald's writing. When questioned, Oswald said he knew no one named Hidell but acknowledged he had been carrying the ID.

Reporters were allowed to ask Oswald questions. The journalists asked whether he had shot Kennedy. He said, "I don't know what dispatches you people have been given, but I emphatically deny these charges."[4] Oswald admitted to being in the building where he worked, but he denied shooting Kennedy. "They've taken me in because of the fact that I lived

Reporters question the arrested Lee Harvey Oswald, *center*, who repeatedly denied killing Kennedy.

in the Soviet Union. I'm just a patsy," Oswald said.[5] Also while in custody, Oswald asked whether John Abt, a prominent lawyer for the Communist Party in the United States, could represent him, but that request never came to fruition.

THE CARCANO RIFLE

The Carcano that Oswald used is a military-grade rifle. The rifle's serial number and a receipt helped investigators discover that Oswald had ordered the rifle through the mail. The Carcano wasn't the fastest rifle to fire or the easiest to operate, but it was inexpensive. Oswald spent less than $13 for the rifle and another $7 for the scope.[6]

On November 24, a group of reporters gathered at the Dallas Police Department to record Oswald being moved to a more secure county jail. As officers led Oswald past reporters, Dallas nightclub owner Jack Ruby stepped out of the crowd and shot Oswald with a revolver. Ruby said he was so angry at Oswald for killing Kennedy that he had to act. Although many people understood this anger, Ruby was charged with murder.

Ruby knew bootleggers and other criminals. Some people believed he was involved in organized crime, specifically the Mafia. These people wondered whether the Mafia had been behind Kennedy's assassination. Kennedy's attorney general, his own brother Robert Kennedy, was cracking down on Mafia leaders. Mafia crime families sold bootleg liquor, operated

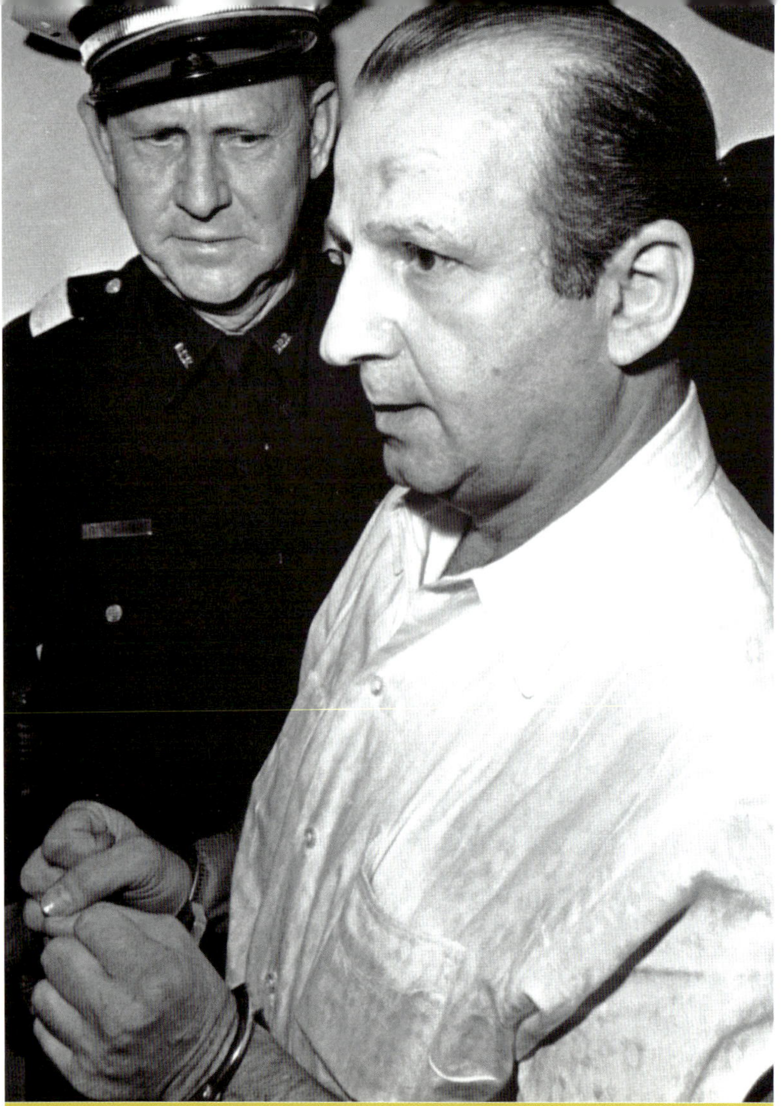

Throughout interviews and his court trial, Jack Ruby, *right*, always maintained that he acted alone in killing Oswald.

illegal gambling rings, and conducted other unlawful business with the goal of gaining money and power. Mafia leaders were known to use illegal means to protect their business, targeting anything or anyone that cost them money, even if that meant killing someone important. Some people speculated that not only had the Mafia worked through Oswald but also that its leaders had told Ruby to keep Oswald from testifying about the role of organized crime in the assassination. However, Dallas police officials who investigated local organized crime never believed this. They thought Ruby bragged too much to be chosen by the Mafia as an accomplice in such a high-profile killing.

Lee Harvey Oswald

Eventually, officials pieced together many facts about Oswald's life. Oswald, who grew up in the Dallas area, started reading about communism when he was about 15 years old. Teachers and his half-brother, John Pic, noted that Oswald seldom connected with others. Oswald dropped out of school at 16 years old. At that time, he tried to enroll in the US Marines but was too young. He later enlisted in 1956, at 17 years old. Fellow Marines said Oswald praised communism and resented taking orders from anyone he considered less intelligent than himself.

RUBY'S TRIAL

During his 1964 trial, Jack Ruby denied that he was guilty of killing Oswald, claiming that he felt so much grief over Kennedy's murder that he had experienced psychomotor epilepsy. According to his attorney, this meant that Ruby had blacked out and shot Oswald subconsciously. However, in March 1964, the jury found Ruby guilty of murder with malice, sentencing him to die in the electric chair. Ruby successfully appealed this verdict in October 1966 when the Texas Court of Criminal Appeals said that Ruby couldn't receive a fair trial in Dallas. Ruby was waiting to be retried when he died of lung cancer in January 1967.

In 1959, after an early discharge from the Marines, Oswald defected to the Soviet Union. This was during the Cold War (1947–1991), when the United States and the Soviet Union competed for allies and built nuclear arsenals in preparation for war. Oswald offered to tell the Soviets everything he had learned as a Marine, but they were unimpressed. They settled him in the quiet city of Minsk as a metal worker in a factory that made radios and televisions. He reportedly had a larger apartment than comparable Soviet workers and an allowance in addition to his salary, but he wanted more. He also continued to resent anyone with authority over him.

On June 1, 1962, Oswald returned to the United States with his wife, Marina, and their newborn daughter. The FBI interviewed Oswald to assess whether he was a security risk, working for the Soviet Union. He promised to let them know if anyone from the Soviet Union asked him to work as a spy. Oswald and his family settled in the Dallas area.

Lee Harvey Oswald couldn't drive, so driving to flee from police was not an option.

On April 10, 1963, Oswald tried to shoot and kill Major General Edwin A. Walker, but his shot missed. Walker, retired from the US Army, was an outspoken anti-Communist, which was probably how he had attracted Oswald's attention.

MAJOR GENERAL EDWIN WALKER

On the night of April 10, 1963, Oswald went to Major General Edwin Walker's Dallas home, where Walker was sitting at his desk, doing his income taxes. At 9:00 p.m., Oswald stood beside a fence, took aim, and fired. The bullet grazed Walker's scalp. When asked by a reporter who might be responsible, Walker said, "There is an enemy within this country."[7] Walker went on to speak against people who wanted to destroy police forces and do away with the US military.

Afterward, Oswald and his wife fled to New Orleans, Louisiana, to avoid being connected to that shooting. No one confirmed that Oswald had tried to shoot Walker until after Kennedy was killed. In trying to shoot Walker, Oswald had used the same rifle that he later used to kill Kennedy.

While he was in New Orleans, Oswald continued to express interest in communism. He organized a New Orleans chapter of Fair Play for Cuba in support of Fidel Castro, the leader of the Communist Party in Cuba. On August 28, 1963, Oswald wrote a letter to the Communist Party USA, asking its central committee for advice.

In September 1963, Oswald traveled to Mexico City and visited both the Soviet and Cuban embassies. He wanted to arrange a visa, the document he would need to travel to Cuba, but no one would give it to him. US intelligence agents noted this trip as suspicious. Meanwhile, Oswald's wife had returned to Dallas and moved in with a friend. Oswald soon returned to Dallas so that he could be near his wife and daughter, and

Lee Harvey Oswald, *right*, and his wife Marina in Russia

he got a job at the Texas School Book Depository. One month later, he shot Kennedy. When interviewed by government investigators after the assassination, Marina Oswald said she didn't think her husband could be happy anywhere. "Only on the moon, perhaps," she said.[8]

The US intelligence community questioned Oswald's alliance after his defection to the Soviet Union, but they couldn't decide if he had worked with the Soviets. Some people worried that Oswald may have been dispatched to the United States by the Soviet Union to kill Kennedy, but the evidence was hardly conclusive. Then, in 1964, Yuri Nosenko, a high-ranking KGB agent, defected to the United States. The KGB was the Soviet Union's secret police force, and Nosenko claimed to be the KGB agent who had kept Oswald's file up to date. Nosenko told the US Central Intelligence Agency (CIA) that the KGB had observed Oswald but did not recruit him. Nosenko also said the Soviet Union played no part in the assassination. He was held and questioned for five years. Cold War experts still argue about whether Nosenko was genuine or a spy sent to cover up Soviet activities in the United States.

THE COLD WAR

After World War II, the Soviet Union and the United States developed a fierce rivalry. As the Soviet Union encouraged other nations to adopt communism, the United States sought to contain communism and threatened nations that allied with the Soviets. After the devastation of World War II, neither side wanted another war of bombs and armies. Instead, they fought a Cold War in which spy networks gathered intelligence on enemies and allies. As the United States and the Soviet Union completely distrusted each other, they each built a stockpile of nuclear weapons. Because of these nuclear arsenals, every political confrontation between the two countries was fraught with the possibility of nuclear war. However, the Cold War ended without nuclear war when the Soviet government collapsed in 1991.

CHAPTER THREE

GATHERING EVIDENCE

When a crime is committed, law enforcement professionals process the crime scene. They gather all of the evidence they can find. This evidence varies from crime to crime. In the case of the Kennedy assassination, the evidence on the sixth floor of the Depository included shell casings, the weapon, and anything else Oswald might have left behind, including fingerprints.

Investigators are meticulous about how they gather evidence. If possible, everything at the crime scene is photographed before it is touched or moved. As the evidence is collected, it is packaged and labeled. That way there is no question that each specific piece of evidence, such as a shell casing or a gun, is the one removed from a specific crime scene. The Dallas police did this when they identified the spent shell casings and the rifle on the sixth floor of the Depository.

Officers gather forensic evidence at the scene of the Kennedy assassination, right outside the Texas School Book Depository.

IGNORING THE CHAIN OF EVIDENCE

Evidence as small as a bullet fragment can be vital during a murder trial. Specialists can tell by the grooves left on a bullet whether it was fired from a particular gun. But if police or agents don't follow the proper procedures while gathering evidence, the evidence cannot be used in court. If a bullet fragment found at the scene of the crime is not photographed in place and labeled, then investigators cannot later prove that it was a particular bullet fragment. So, even if a bullet is determined to have been fired from the suspect's gun, it can't be used in court if it was not properly documented. In the case of the Kennedy assassination, bullets pocketed by Secret Service agents without being labeled could not be admitted as evidence in court.

Evidence found outside of the crime scene, such as a bullet removed from a patient at the hospital, should also be labeled and packaged as soon as possible.

Gathering evidence can be tricky. Sometimes, crime scene technicians have to be careful not to damage or lose evidence. For example, lifting a fingerprint from a doorknob means that the oils that create the print are lifted. After this process, the print on the doorknob is no longer clear and cannot be taken again. Collecting fingerprint evidence has to be done right the first time.

If evidence is not properly labeled, people may question whether the items in hand are the ones that were collected at the crime scene. They may question whether evidence was switched or planted to make a particular person look guilty or innocent. In the case of the Kennedy assassination, evidence was not always gathered carefully, which has fed some conspiracy theories concerning Kennedy's death.

The Presidential Limousine

At Parkland Memorial Hospital, after Agent Paul Landis helped Jackie Kennedy from the limousine, he spotted a bullet fragment on the car. To keep the fragment from being lost, he picked it up and put it on the seat. He also admitted to seeing the president's lighter (recognizable because it was decorated

A bullet cracked the windshield of Kennedy's limousine. With this and other evidence, the car itself was considered a crime scene.

WHAT HAPPENED TO THE LIMOUSINE?

Kennedy's customized limousine had two removable roofs (one plastic and one metal), running boards, and two radio telephones. This limousine would cost $1.5 million today and was too expensive to simply crush, store, or sell after the assassination. After investigators were done with the car, White House staff cleaned it thoroughly. Then steel armor panels, bulletproof glass, and a permanent roof were added. The engine was modified for more power, and the car was painted. President Johnson didn't want to be seen driving around in a car that was clearly the limousine from Kennedy's last motorcade. The car was used for 13 more years following the assassination.[1]

with the presidential seal), picking it up, and putting it in his pocket for safe keeping. Both of these items were evidence, and Landis moved them before they were cataloged.

The limousine was part of a crime scene and should have been treated as such. This means it should have been cordoned off with yellow police tape until a forensic specialist could inspect the scene. Photographs should have been taken of the blood splatter patterns. A technician should have taken samples of the blood and other materials. Bullets and bullet fragments should also have been gathered at this time. But before any of that could happen, it appears the limousine was cleaned.

Some hospital staff members reportedly said a man dressed in a suit entered the hospital and asked for a bucket of water and towels. "The implication was that they were going to clean out the car—clean out the crime scene," says Gary Mack, who has researched the Kennedy assassination as curator of the Sixth Floor Museum at Dealey Plaza.[2] If someone was trying to clean the car, however, they failed to do a thorough job. Working in a Secret Service garage in Washington, DC, investigators spent a month gathering skull and bullet fragments, removing the windshield with the bullet hole, and cleaning the upholstery.

The Autopsy

Failing to properly process the limousine evidence wasn't investigators' only mistake. By law, Dr. Earl Rose, the Dallas County medical examiner, should have conducted an autopsy on Kennedy's body. An autopsy is a medical examination of a dead body, internally and externally, to determine how the person died. Doctors often cut into the body to remove tissue for testing or to view specific organs to assess damage or health. In the case of a murder, the autopsy is a way to gather evidence. This evidence is recorded through X-rays, photographs, measurements, and observation. In an autopsy for a shooting victim, a skilled medical examiner

The Kennedy limousine can now be seen on display in the Henry Ford Museum in Dearborn, Michigan.

JURISDICTIONAL DISPUTES

When an agency has the authority to make decisions and investigate a specific crime, they have jurisdiction. In the United States, there are many types of agencies with overlapping jurisdictions. At the national level are the federal agencies such as the Secret Service and the FBI. There are also state police, such as Texas state troopers, and various forms of law enforcement at the county level, such as departments that operate under elected sheriffs, including the Dallas County Sheriff's Department. There are also city police forces, such as the Dallas Police Department. With the many layers of law enforcement, it can be difficult to determine which agency has jurisdiction—and, therefore, the power to investigate—regarding a specific crime.

can tell from which direction a bullet hit. The photos, X-rays, and a variety of paperwork record the evidence in ways that preserve the information for investigation and to be used in court.

The Secret Service had no intention of letting Dr. Rose autopsy the president. They wanted to get Kennedy's body back to Washington, DC, as soon as possible. Local officials were still trying to argue about this with Secret Service agents when the agents put the coffin carrying Kennedy's body into a hearse. They wanted him to be autopsied in Washington, DC.

As they were leaving the hospital, Agent Dick Johnsen was approached by a hospital staff member. Someone had found a spent bullet on Connally's stretcher. Johnsen saw that the bullet had been fired. Instead of immediately labeling this piece of evidence with his initials, he wrapped it in his handkerchief and put it in his pocket. The chain of evidence was again broken.

Air Force One, the president's airplane, was in flight back to Washington, DC, when Jackie Kennedy decided that her husband should be taken to Bethesda Naval Hospital in Maryland because he had been in the US Navy. There, Kennedy was autopsied by Dr. James Humes and Dr. Thornton Boswell, navy officers and pathologists who were experts on how disease affects the human body. They knew how to do

Air Force One carrying Kennedy's coffin arrives at Andrews Air Force Base in Maryland.

UNRELIABLE EYEWITNESSES

While trying to solve a crime, investigators talk to eyewitnesses—people who may have seen or heard something important. However, eyewitnesses aren't always reliable. Part of the problem is the way human memory works. When a person remembers something, his or her memory doesn't play it back like a video. According to memory researcher and psychologist Elizabeth F. Loftus of the University of California, Irvine, remembering something is more like rebuilding a puzzle. Each person only remembers bits and pieces of an event and will have to reassemble the memory to discuss it with investigators. During this reassembly, things the person has forgotten will be left out. Other times, an incorrect piece, which could be provided when an investigator asks a leading question, will be included. This is part of the reason why no two people have the same memories of a single event.

a medical autopsy, which checks to see whether and how a disease or medical condition killed someone. But they were not experts in conducting forensic autopsies, which can tell not only how a person died (for example, traumatic injury) but also what caused that injury (such as a bullet passing from front to back or back to front).

Because they had not been trained in forensics, the navy doctors did not ask for Kennedy's clothing, which should have been part of what they examined. Eventually, they concluded that he was hit by two bullets from above and behind, but they failed to note the point of entry for the head wound. There is a photograph of the back of Kennedy's head, but his hair was not shaved off, so it obscures the entry wound. This lack of hard evidence fueled controversy for years to come. Did the shot actually come from a sixth-floor window? A clearly defined entry wound would have helped answer this question.

Misidentifications

In addition to evidence not being properly documented from the crime scenes and not collected during the autopsy, authorities made mistakes and misstatements to the public about key pieces of evidence. Though they later corrected these misstatements, when authorities change what they say during the course of an investigation, it can cast doubt on the findings. All eyes were on Dallas after Kennedy was assassinated. The police responded to the stress by making frequent statements to the press. The information they gave was not always accurate.

The night after the assassination, Secret Service agents discussed the possibilities of a conspiracy involving the Mafia, Cuba, or the Soviet Union.

One error concerned Oswald's rifle. When it was found in the Depository, one deputy mistakenly called it a Mauser, which is a different type of rifle. This deputy had not seen the rifle up close. From a distance, the rifle resembled, in his opinion, a Mauser. The Carcano was not a very common rifle, so this mistake is not surprising, but even today people wonder whether at some point police swapped one

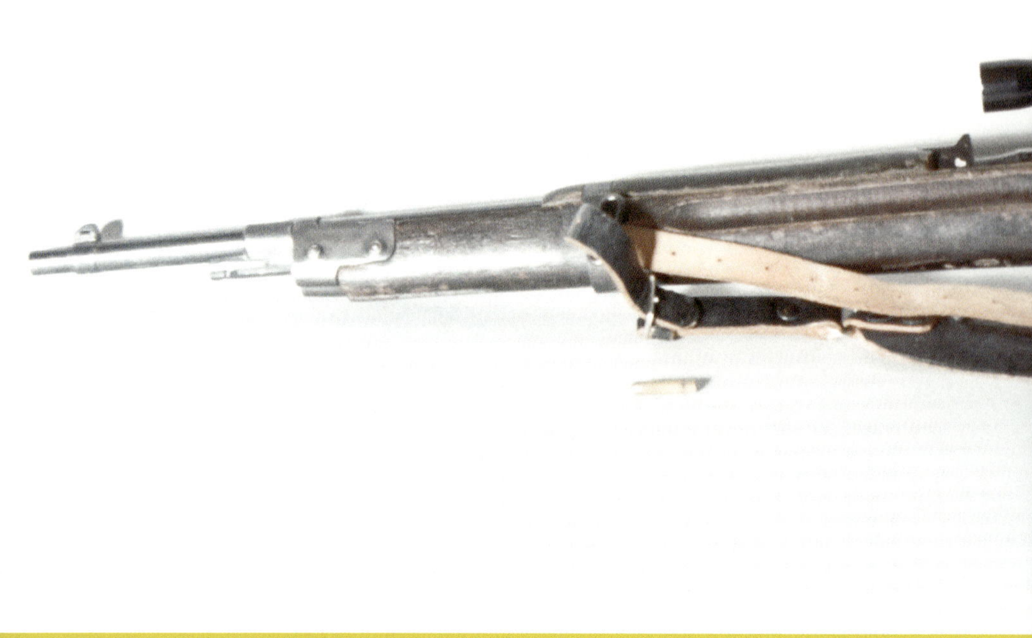

Investigators identified the Carcano rifle used to kill Kennedy.

gun for another or whether more than one rifle was involved in the assassination.

Another error involved chicken bones found on the sixth floor of the Depository. Police informed the press that they were the remains of Oswald's lunch. They said he had eaten while waiting for the motorcade to pass. However, investigators later determined that another Depository employee, one of the men who heard the shooting while watching Kennedy's motorcade from the fifth floor, had eaten his lunch and left

his trash on the sixth floor before joining his coworkers one floor below.

To many people, these discrepancies seem minor. But they are enough to cause skeptics to question the evidence. It is from this doubt that conspiracy theories are born. Today, there are theories about multiple shooters and rifles. These cause some people to question who really shot Kennedy.

CHAPTER FOUR

THE WARREN COMMISSION

Once he became president, Lyndon Johnson could have immediately created a commission to investigate Kennedy's assassination. But the FBI was already investigating. President Johnson believed this agency would do the job well.

Not everyone agreed that this was the best course of action, however. Johnson received phone calls from several influential people who pushed him to launch an investigation. The callers included Joe Alsop, a columnist at the *Washington Post* newspaper; Eugene Rostow, dean of the Yale Law School; and Dean Acheson, the US secretary of state from 1949 to 1953. The US Department of State handles international relations, and during the Cold War this meant working to limit the spread and influence of communism. In addition to these phone calls, Johnson learned that both the House of Representatives and

Lyndon B. Johnson, *right*, was sworn in as president the day Kennedy died.

CONSPIRACY THEORISTS LOOK AT JOHNSON

Johnson and Kennedy had a rocky relationship, paired together on a political ticket but incompatible in every other way. Kennedy was posh and polished. Johnson took pride in his rough Texas roots. During an interview, Jackie Kennedy revealed that her husband was so worried about what Johnson might do if he became president that Kennedy was talking to important people in politics about blocking Johnson's expected 1968 campaign for the presidency, which would have come after a second Kennedy administration. Conspiracy theorists think that Johnson decided to not only block this move by Kennedy but also get into the presidency ahead of schedule. They believe Johnson did this by having Kennedy killed while in Johnson's home state. Johnson's allies, according to this theory, were men who had gotten rich in oil and were afraid that Kennedy would cut the government allowances they received for drilling and developing new oil wells.

the Senate were discussing forming separate commissions to investigative the assassination.

On November 29, 1963, a week after becoming president, Johnson established the President's Commission on the Assassination of President Kennedy. The group would come to be known as the Warren Commission. The commission was made up of seven people: Supreme Court chief justice Earl Warren, who was chairman of the commission, Senators Richard Russell and John Sherman Cooper, Representatives Gerald Ford and Hale Boggs, former CIA director Allen Dulles, and Council on Foreign Relations chairman John McCloy. Members of the commission were carefully selected because Johnson wanted the group to represent all parts of the federal government.

Not everyone Johnson selected considered it an honor. When Warren was asked to chair the commission, he repeatedly turned Johnson down. Warren only agreed when Johnson told him that an incomplete or poorly managed report would lead to public panic and maybe even cause a nuclear war with Communist nations. This was at the height of the Cold War, and US government leaders believed the Communist threat could not be overlooked. They also worried that if the Soviet Union had been involved in the assassination, the public might demand retaliation against the Soviets. And during the Cold War, officials worried that any military retaliation might lead to a nuclear war.

SUPREME COURT CHIEF JUSTICE EARL WARREN

Warren was a railroad worker before he graduated from the University of California, Berkeley, with a law degree in 1914. After serving stateside in the Army during World War I (1914–1918), he worked as a deputy district attorney. In 1926, Warren won election as the district attorney of Alameda County, California. He became well known for his stance against corruption and was elected as California's governor in 1942, 1946, and 1950. He was appointed to the US Supreme Court in 1953 by President Dwight D. Eisenhower. In 1954, he delivered the Supreme Court's unanimous decision in *Brown v. Board of Education of Topeka*, which determined that segregation of schools by race was unconstitutional. Warren said the corruption and exploitation of the workers he had seen during his time on the railroad led him to fight corruption and exploitation as an attorney and judge.

Senator Richard Russell wanted to avoid serving on the committee entirely. He didn't approve of Warren's record as a liberal court justice. Johnson ignored this refusal and included Russell because it was "for the good of America."[1] Johnson may not have originally seen a need for the commission, but once he decided to organize it, he was determined to recruit members he thought would calm public fears.

Examining the Facts

In conducting their investigation, the members of the commission interviewed 550 witnesses.[2] They also examined documents and other pieces of evidence and even visited Dallas. However, investigating the assassination of President Kennedy was such a monumental task that the commission's seven members could not do it alone. To aid in their investigation, the committee acquired a full staff, including a general counsel, or head lawyer, 14 assistant counsels, Internal Revenue Service agents, a historian, an editor, and various assistants. As the commission conducted its work, it requested help and information from various agencies in Texas and within the federal government.

The commission reviewed reports by the FBI, the Secret Service, the Department of State, and the Texas attorney general's office, which is the state's chief legal office. Among the files that the commission examined was information the FBI gathered on Oswald. Oswald had come to the attention of the FBI when he defected to the Soviet Union. The FBI didn't think he had any valuable information that he might reveal to the Soviets, but agents worried that with his return to the United States he might be spying for this foreign power.

Upon his return, Oswald was interviewed by two FBI agents. They decided he wasn't a threat at that time.

Lee Harvey Oswald, *right*, and his wife, Marina, spend time with their daughter in the Soviet Union before moving their family to the United States.

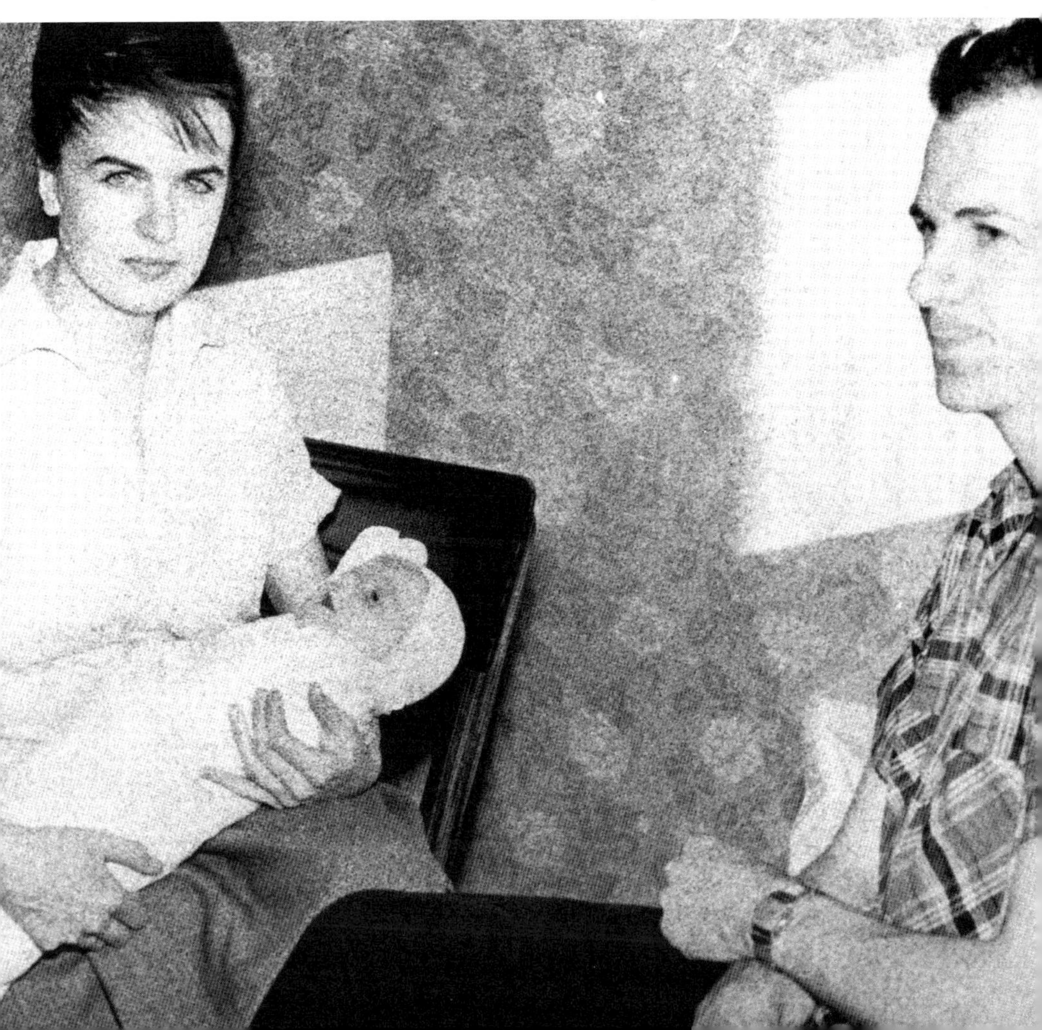

They later gathered information in regard to his work for Fair Play for Cuba in New Orleans. Oswald was the only New Orleans member of Fair Play for Cuba, but he used the name of the group to get media interviews and hand out fliers. Oswald's work on Fair Play for Cuba was another reason some investigators thought he might have ties to the Soviet Union. Several times when he was interviewed, Oswald lied to agents about small details, such as when and where he and his wife, Marina, had married. However, the FBI found no evidence he was spying for the Soviets. The commission also interviewed people who knew Oswald personally. They talked to his wife and his brother, Robert Edward Lee Oswald. Among other things, his brother talked about how often they had moved as children.

The commission also interviewed people connected to Kennedy. William Robert Greer was driving Kennedy's limousine at the time of the assassination. The commission questioned Greer about how fast he had been driving. Greer noted that he liked to keep four or five car lengths between the limousine and the next car in case he needed to put on a burst of speed. They also interviewed fingerprint experts, people who had witnessed the assassination, ballistics experts who could testify about firearms, and more.

Commission members also reviewed letters, receipts, and photographs. Evidence gathered by the commission was detailed in 26 published volumes. However, despite this vast amount of information, there was some evidence that the full commission was not allowed to see. Warren refused to allow commission members to view photographs taken during Kennedy's autopsy. He said the images were too disturbing. He also tried, but failed, to keep the commission from interviewing Jackie Kennedy. He said he didn't want to invade her privacy, especially when she was mourning her husband. Some people believe that Warren was trying to protect the Kennedys, as he was a friend of the family. They think he may have had too personal a relationship to be objective in the investigation. But Warren wasn't the only one who withheld information. The CIA and FBI withheld information as well. For example, the CIA was aware of Oswald's visit to the Cuban embassy in Mexico City when he made the trip. The agency later lied to the Warren Commission about this fact, with CIA officials stating they only learned about this visit after the assassination.

The printed Warren Report is 888 pages long.[3]

Conclusions

The commission published its findings in a report that can now be found online and at the US National Archives in

Earl Warren, *left*, hands the completed Warren Report to President Johnson in September 1964.

Washington, DC. In the Warren Report, the commission concluded that Oswald, from the Texas School Book Depository, fired the bullets that injured Connally and killed Kennedy. No evidence was found that either Oswald or Ruby were part of a Communist or organized crime conspiracy. Although the report also described Oswald's life prior to the assassination in great detail, including his time in the Soviet Union, it did not speculate about his motive for killing the president.

The commission also concluded that the Secret Service did a poor job in preparing for Kennedy's visit to Dallas and in protecting him once he was there. The commission members did not simply blame the men protecting Kennedy when he was assassinated; they acknowledged that keeping the president safe was incredibly difficult because presidents did not always take the recommendations of the Secret Service seriously. But four presidents—Abraham Lincoln, James Garfield, William McKinley, and Kennedy—had been assassinated in the previous 100 years, so the government clearly needed to take steps to prevent this from happening again.

During a 1966 interview, Johnson told journalist Walter Cronkite that he could not be certain a foreign power wasn't responsible for Kennedy's assassination.

The report pointed out that the route planned for Kennedy's Dallas visit had been primarily examined by a single agent. This agent noted that there were safer routes that would keep the motorcade on the highway and moving fast, but these routes were not compatible with Kennedy's goals for being seen and interacting with citizens. The commission found that the Secret Service should have communicated with local law

"A CRUEL AND SHOCKING ACT"

The Warren Report, published by the US Government Printing Office, opened with a statement concerning why the commission was needed:

> *The assassination of John Fitzgerald Kennedy on November 22, 1963, was a cruel and shocking act of violence directed against a man, a family, a nation, and against all mankind. A young and vigorous leader whose years of public and private life stretched before him was the victim. . . . This Commission was created on November 29, 1963, in recognition of the right of people everywhere to full and truthful knowledge concerning these events.*[5]

The commission, according to this statement, conducted its work based on reason and fairness.

enforcement to cover tall buildings and other locations that could be used by a sniper to ambush the president.

There had been no foreign Communist plot. Organized crime was not involved. But the Secret Service, according to the commission, needed to be stronger, and there needed to be better procedures in place for keeping the president safe.

Initially, the Warren Report seemed to do what Johnson had hoped, soothing the worries of the American public concerning Kennedy's assassination. A few months after the report was published, a Gallup poll showed that 87 percent of those polled believed that Oswald was the shooter.[4] Then, in 1966, lawyer Mark Lane published the book *Rush to Judgment*, a critique of the commission that became a best seller and fueled conspiracy theories about the assassination. Ironically, there is also a conspiracy theory about *Rush to Judgment*. In their book *The Sword and the Shield*, authors Christopher Andrew and Vasili Mitrokhin claim that Lane received money from the KGB to help with research for his book. If Andrew and Mitrokhin are correct, then by helping Lane complete his book, the KGB helped encourage conspiracy theories and unrest in the United States. When another Gallup poll was taken in 1966, only 36 percent of those surveyed were still convinced that Oswald had acted alone.[6]

CHAPTER FIVE

THE ZAPRUDER FILM

Some of the photographs reviewed by the Warren Commission were still images taken from the Zapruder film. The Zapruder film is a home movie that shows the assassination happening. It was not the only movie filmed by a witness that day, but it was the most complete.

On the day of the assassination, Abraham Zapruder, a 58-year-old Dallas business owner, was in Dealey Plaza with his new movie camera to film Kennedy's motorcade as it drove by. Zapruder was born in Russia, part of the Soviet Union, but he moved to the United States as a teen. After learning garment manufacturing as a patternmaker in Brooklyn, New York, Zapruder moved to Texas with his wife.

The camera used by Zapruder has been displayed at the Newseum, a museum dedicated to journalism, in Washington, DC.

DUAL ELECTRIC
f/1.8
Bell & Howell
Zoom Lens
Varamat
Bell & How
ZOOMATIC

There, he established a clothing company that included a dress line specifically for teens. His office was across the street from the Depository. Zapruder and his receptionist went to Dealey Plaza to see the president, but he hadn't planned to take his new camera, a Bell and Howell Model 414PD Zoomatic Director Series camera, until his assistant encouraged him to do so. Unlike many along the motorcade's route, Zapruder had found a slightly elevated place to stand, a concrete block, so he was able to get a good view of the motorcade. He used his camera's zoom lens to film a close-up view.

Caught on Film

The Zapruder film is only 26 seconds long, but it shows the Kennedy assassination in full color.[1] Zapruder's focus through the entire film was the presidential limousine, which is seen

OTHER FILMS

There are at least three other films of the assassination, but they are all shorter or less clear than the Zapruder film. Brief films from different angles and vantage points were made by Marie Muchmore and Mark Bell. Charles Bronson took several photographs and two seconds of film that show Jackie Kennedy moving onto the limousine's trunk. Bronson's film was shot farther back from the car than Zapruder's. It shows more of the plaza and also the car full of Secret Service agents. Because of this, his film disproves the conspiracy theory that a Secret Service agent in the car behind Kennedy accidentally shot and killed the president.

with two police motorcycles behind and to the left. The car carrying the Secret Service agents can be seen directly behind the president's car. The limousine is briefly out of sight as it passes behind a sign.

As the limo comes back into view, Kennedy is clutching his throat. At this point, the viewer can see Jackie Kennedy, in her raspberry-colored suit, lean forward to help her husband, who has been shot through his neck. Then he is struck again. This shot to his head is obvious in the movie. Immediately after the shot, the viewer can see Jackie Kennedy pulling herself onto the trunk of the car even as Agent Hill pulls himself up from behind. The limousine disappears behind trees or bushes as Hill pushes the First Lady back into the car.

Just minutes after the shooting, *Dallas Morning News* reporter Darwin Payne asked to interview Zapruder. In an

NOT VIDEO

When Zapruder filmed the presidential motorcade, his camera captured a series of images by exposing film to light. The film then had to be chemically developed and an exposure, like a photographic print, made so that it could be viewed. Four hundred and eighty-six frames make up the Zapruder film, which runs just over 26 seconds. When the frames are played back, they look like a single moving image. But there are short gaps in time between each frame. Unlike film, a digital recording is a single continuous video that can be viewed immediately. It also captures events from start to finish without missing fractions of seconds, as happens with film.

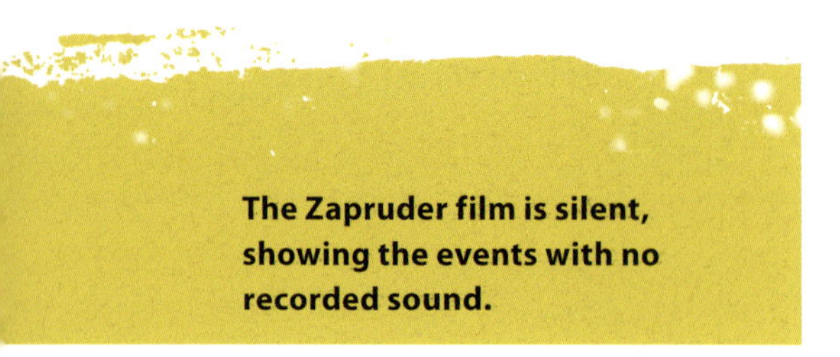

The Zapruder film is silent, showing the events with no recorded sound.

hour-long interview, Zapruder cried as he recounted what he had seen. Payne encouraged Zapruder to have the film developed, but Zapruder was determined to hand it over to the authorities. As the two spoke, they watched Walter Cronkite on the TV news. Cronkite initially reported that Kennedy had been injured, but Zapruder told Payne this was wrong. "I know he's dead. I was watching through the viewfinder," Zapruder told Payne.[2]

Zapruder and Secret Service agent Forrest Sorrels had the film developed at the Eastman Kodak processing plant in Dallas. Three copies, called exposures, were made. Zapruder handed two of these over to the Secret Service. Zapruder sold the original film to *Life* magazine for $150,000, which would be more than $1 million today.[3]

Key Frame Withheld

When Zapruder sold rights to the film to *Life* magazine, he did so knowing they would publish single frames as photos. But part of the agreement was that they would not publish Frame 313, the single image that captured when Kennedy was shot in his head. Zapruder explained that he still had nightmares from what he had seen and did not want to expose Americans to the horror.

Life published 31 black-and-white images in its regular weekly magazine, the next issue after the assassination.[4] Two weeks later, some of the photos were printed in color in a special memorial issue of the magazine. When *Life* magazine was working with the original film, the film was damaged and pieced back together. These repaired places, called splices, can be clearly seen in the original film. The magazine released a statement in early 1967 stating that four frames of film had been accidentally destroyed by a *Life* photo lab technician in 1963. Conspiracy theorists believe that the CIA forged the film to show there was only one gunman, which these theorists believe is a lie.

ZAPRUDER CRITICIZED

People criticized Zapruder for selling *Life* the rights to his film. He chose *Life* because it was a leading magazine. He hoped it would do the tragedy justice, handling the film as news and not something sensational. *Life* executives regretted buying the film. They did not want to license it, or sell permission to use images from the film to another company. To do so would likely put photos of a tragedy on products such as posters or tote bags. The company eventually sold the film back to the Zapruder family for $1.00. The family placed the film in the National Archives and allowed it to be viewed there only by certain people. When the federal government said it would publicly release the film in 1992, the family refused. They felt the film was too disturbing to be readily accessible. The government then purchased the film for $16 million and has released it in full. The Zapruder family is still criticized for profiting, although today people regularly sell video to news outlets.[5]

Life magazine, along with other publications at the time, printed a special memorial issue honoring President Kennedy after he was assassinated.

In 1968, *Life* hired a film lab to make copies of the Zapruder film. Moses Weitzman, general manager of technical animations, made several copies of the film. He screened them to see which was the highest quality and gave that one to *Life*. Instead of destroying the other copies, he kept them. One of his employees, Robert Groden, also copied the film in 1969. Working with this copy, he enhanced it to remove shakiness and to make it clearer.

In 1975, Geraldo Rivera, an ABC News reporter, got one of Groden's bootleg copies of the film. Rivera convinced executives to allow him to show the film on his weekly talk show, *Good Night America*. That March 6, 1975, show was the first time the American public had the opportunity to see full-color footage of Kennedy being shot. Rivera ended his program that night with a challenge to the US government to make an intensive, official investigation beyond the investigations that had already been conducted by the Warren Commission and the FBI.

Millions of people saw the full Zapruder film on *Good Night America*. They saw Kennedy's head jerk backward as he was shot. They had been told by the Warren Commission and other authorities that

RIVERA'S TAKE

Years after the assassination, in 2017, a Fox News contributor asked Geraldo Rivera whether he believed that there was a conspiracy or whether Oswald alone had shot Kennedy. Rivera said he thought people simply did not want to think someone like a president could be brought down by Oswald, whom he described as a "banal, selfish, egotistical, narcissistic punk." Rivera said, "You want more. You want it to be a conspiracy. You want a perpetrator who is of equal stature to the monumental nature of the crime."[6]

THE UMBRELLA MAN

November 22, 1963, started out rainy, but by noon the sky was clear and sunny. However, the Zapruder film and various still photos show a man standing under a big black umbrella next to the highway sign where the limousine was when the shots began. Some conspiracy theorists believed that the umbrella framework included a hollow tube used to aim and shoot either a poison dart or flechette, a heavy dart shot by a gun, into Kennedy's neck. In 1978, Louie David Witt came forward to a House of Representatives committee and admitted that he was the Umbrella Man. He had carried a black umbrella as a protest. He was protesting a policy that Kennedy's grandfather, Ambassador Joseph Kennedy, had supported before World War II. The committee accepted this explanation, although critics claim Witt provided no evidence, other than a black umbrella, that he was the man in the photographs.

he was shot from behind but couldn't reconcile that with the image they saw on TV.

When the American people saw the complete footage, they were largely primed to believe that the government, through the Warren Commission, had lied to them. After all, at the time the video aired on *Good Night America*, it had been less than one year since President Richard Nixon's 1974 resignation due to his role in the Watergate scandal, which involved a break-in at the Democratic National Committee headquarters in Washington, DC. During this break-in, several men were arrested while trying to illegally place wiretaps in the headquarters. Evidence showed that Nixon may have known of and even authorized the burglary. Facing impeachment, which could result in removal from the office of president, Nixon resigned.

Additionally, another investigation had led the public to doubt US intelligence agencies shortly before the full Zapruder film was released. In January 1975, the Senate Select Committee to Study Governmental Operations with Respect to Intelligence Activities was formed under the leadership of Senator Frank Church, an Idaho Democrat. Known as the Church Committee, this group investigated various US intelligence organizations and their surveillance of US citizens. One of the questions the committee asked regarded what information government agencies could collect without a search warrant. The committee found that during investigations, US intelligence agencies had regularly ignored the Constitution and laws limiting their actions, resulting in these agencies sometimes opening people's mail and placing wiretaps on the phones of American citizens. The committee's investigation marked the need to balance individual freedoms with national security. With these recent events in mind, when Americans saw the Zapruder film, many demanded to know what the Warren Commission had covered up.

Zapruder is often considered a pioneer of citizen journalism, an ordinary person who captured an important event.

CHAPTER SIX

A COMMITTEE ON ASSASSINATIONS

The American public's trust in the government had diminished for several reasons. The Church Committee had revealed that not only had US intelligence agencies spied on American citizens, but the CIA had also allegedly plotted to assassinate foreign leaders. And after seeing the Zapruder film, people wanted answers about the Kennedy assassination, too. Books about conspiracy theories encouraged people to ask questions and demand to know what had really happened.

In response, the House of Representatives voted to create the House Select Committee on Assassinations in September 1976 to reinvestigate the assassinations of Kennedy and civil rights leader Martin Luther King Jr., who was shot to death on April 4, 1968. The committee was composed of 12 representatives and included two subcommittees: one

Richard Sprague, chief lawyer to the House Select Committee on Assassinations, speaks with committee members during their first meeting in 1976.

DR. MARTIN LUTHER KING JR.

Dr. Martin Luther King Jr. (1929–1968) was a social activist who believed in peaceful protest and led the American civil rights movement for nearly 15 years. King led marches, sit-ins, and boycotts to protest segregation and inequality. He is known for leading the Montgomery Bus Boycott (December 1955–December 1956), which led the US Supreme Court to declare segregated seating on public transit unconstitutional. He also led the March on Washington (August 1963) during which 200,000 to 300,000 protesters gathered before the Lincoln Memorial to hear King's now-famous "I Have a Dream" speech.[3] In 1964, King became the youngest person to win the Nobel Peace Prize. On April 4, 1968, King was in Memphis to support a sanitation worker's strike when he was shot and killed. Known racist and escaped convict James Earl Ray pleaded guilty to killing King and was convicted and sentenced to 99 years in prison, although he later recanted his confession.

to investigate the Kennedy assassination and the other to investigate King's.[1] The committee had four goals, starting with confirming the identities of the assassins who had killed Kennedy and King. The committee also investigated whether the assassins had acted alone or whether they had help in implementing the assassinations. Third, the committee wanted to know whether various agencies within the US government had adequately performed their duties in collecting and sharing information both before and while investigating Kennedy's assassination. Fourth, the committee would decide if laws needed to be changed or created to stop another political assassination from happening.

What They Examined

The House Select Committee members worked with a team of 170 lawyers, investigators, and researchers.[2] They sought out any information having to do with the assassinations. This meant that they were frequently reexamining evidence that had been reviewed by the Warren Commission. Sometimes, they were looking at it simply to see whether the investigative work had been thorough and correct the first time, meaning the evidence was properly gathered and examined and the autopsy was done correctly. Other times, the House Select Committee examined old evidence using new scientific techniques or with the goal of proving or disproving a specific conspiracy theory.

From the beginning, the committee struggled internally. Members left, including the original chairman, Congressman Thomas Nelms Downing. The new chairman, Congressman Henry Gonzalez, then fired the committee's head lawyer. In addition, the committee received criticism about how much money it was spending in its investigations. Despite these problems, the investigations proceeded, lasting approximately two years.

The committee had a nine-doctor forensic pathology panel to review Kennedy's autopsy. The panel examined the X-rays and photographs and also interviewed the doctors involved. It concluded that Kennedy had been shot twice from above and behind. One bullet hit him in his upper back and exited his throat, while another fatally struck him in his head. These findings agreed with what the Warren Commission had stated in its report.

Many photographs had been used as evidence in the Warren Commission investigations. The House Committee brought in photographic experts to evaluate the images. In part, they aimed to answer a specific question. Were all of the images in the photographs real, or had they somehow been faked?

Among the photographs that the committee studied of Oswald was one of him taken when he served in the US Marine Corps.

One of the most contentious photographs showed Oswald standing in his backyard, holding the Carcano rifle. Oswald had denied that he was the person shown in the photo. Experts had to decide whether the photographed man was indeed Oswald and whether the rifle he held was the same one found at the Depository. The experts concluded that the rifle in the photo with Oswald was the rifle found in the Depository. It was also the rifle photographed by some eyewitnesses to the assassination and later in police evidence. The experts explained that in some photos the rifle seemed to be a different length but that this was a result of the angle at which the photo had been taken. They also determined that it was Oswald in the photo.

This famous image of Lee Harvey Oswald, known commonly as the "backyard photo," has been heavily questioned, but experts have determined the man is Oswald and he is holding the gun he used to shoot Kennedy.

THE SECOND OSWALD

One of the conspiracy theories investigated by the House Select Committee was the theory that there were two Lee Harvey Oswalds. Conspiracy theorists believe that when Lee Harvey Oswald returned to the United States from Russia, he was not the real Lee Harvey Oswald. They believe he was a Soviet plant who had been sent back to the United States to take Oswald's place and to eventually kill Kennedy. To investigate this particular theory, the House Select Committee collected and examined photos of Oswald, some from before he went to Russia and some from after his return. The committee concluded that the Lee Harvey Oswald who went to the Soviet Union was the same man as the Lee Harvey Oswald who returned to the United States. There was no second Oswald.

The experts also examined the photos of Kennedy's autopsy. Calvin McCamy, a photogrammetrist, testified before the committee. Photogrammetry is the science of taking measurements based on a photo. Studying paired images, each showing similar things from a different angle, McCamy could tell that the photos were genuine.

Perhaps the most controversial piece of evidence was a dictabelt recording. A Dictaphone used a needle to record sound patterns on broad loops of flexible plastic called dictabelts. The Dictaphone was hooked up to either a telephone or a two-way radio set to record conversations. On the day of the assassination, a motorcycle officer had left his radio microphone on, transmitting all of the sounds around him. These sounds were then recorded on the dictabelt.

To simply listen to it, the roar of the motorcycle drowned out all other noise. This had not been an issue for the Warren Commission because the commission's members had read transcripts of the police radio recordings, noting what the police had said, but they did not listen to the recordings themselves. The House Committee had two different labs attempt to clarify the background sounds on the recordings. At least four different spikes in volume were found that were consistent with the spikes that would come from gunshots.

The House Committee then conducted experiments in Dealey Plaza, positioning microphones and recording the sounds of rifle shots from various positions. One shot from a specific position along the fence on a nearby grassy knoll matched one of the recorded sound spikes on the dictabelt. The committee decided that this was evidence of a fourth shot.

Committee Conclusions

The findings of the House Select Committee on Assassinations agreed with those of the Warren Commission in several important areas. The House Committee agreed that Kennedy had not received sufficient protection when he was in Dallas. The committee also stated that Oswald had shot at Kennedy three times. The first shot missed, the second hit but did not kill him, and the third hit and killed Kennedy.

But there were also several key areas in which the two reports differed. Based on the dictabelt, the House Committee concluded that a fourth shot had been fired. Since Oswald had only fired three shots, this meant that a second gunman had been present. The committee also said that the evidence convinced them there had most likely been a conspiracy, meaning that Oswald had not been acting alone but as an agent of some larger power. Although they could not determine what power had been behind Oswald's actions, they did not think it was the Soviet Union, Cuba, the Mafia, or the CIA. Given these findings, it isn't surprising that the House Committee also concluded that the Warren Commission had done a poor job investigating, in part because its findings were too definitive.

After these findings were made public, the dictabelt recording was reexamined in 1982. This time, experts said the recording did not include the sounds of gunshots. The committee's evaluation of the recording had been incorrect. There was no fourth shot. There was no second shooter. From the start of the investigation, the police officer whose radio was open stated that he had not been in a position where he could have heard the gunshots. In addition, the gunshot-like sounds

NOT UNANIMOUS

When the forensics pathology panel concluded that Kennedy had been struck by only two bullets, one doctor disagreed. It was Dr. Cyril H. Wecht, the coroner of Allegheny County in Pennsylvania. When the Zapruder film showed Kennedy's head flung back, Wecht agreed with people who felt this indicated a shot from the right. He believed this bullet, from the side, struck at the same time as the one from the rear but disintegrated completely. The other panelists disagreed, calling Wecht's suspicion speculation because none of them knew of any bullet that could actually do this. They also believed that a second head wound would have been visible in the X-rays or photographs.

occurred in the recording after Kennedy's motorcade was on its way to the hospital.

The House Committee was also criticized by various agents from within the US government. Eldon J. Rudd, a former FBI agent who had investigated Kennedy's assassination, stated that the committee "fanned the flames of rumor, distortion and unwanted distrust of law enforcement agencies." By issuing a report that was later shown to include incorrect conclusions, the committee hadn't reassured the American public. It had done the opposite.

CHAPTER SEVEN

FIFTY YEARS LATER

In 2013, 50 years after Kennedy was killed, Americans continued to question the government's investigations, wondering what really happened when the president was shot. The producers of *NOVA*, a prime-time PBS television show about science and engineering, decided to find out what science could reveal about how Kennedy died. They brought in specialists to use modern research techniques, including ballistics, laser mapping, and sound studies to reexamine the assassination.

Ballistics Basics

Two ballistics experts went to a shooting range with a 6.5 mm Carcano rifle identical to the one used by Oswald. Ballistics experts know how a bullet moves when it is fired, spinning, tumbling, or falling. They also know what happens when this

An *X* permanently marks the spot in Dealey Plaza where Kennedy was shot. Tourists visit the landmark.

bullet strikes a target. Luke Haag has 50 years of experience as a ballistics expert and was the director of the Phoenix Crime Laboratory in Phoenix, Arizona. His son, Michael Haag, is also an expert and works for the Albuquerque Police Crime Lab in New Mexico. He also teaches shooting reconstruction, which is how to look at the physical evidence and reconstruct what happened during a shooting.

The bullet from Oswald's Carcano would have left the rifle at 2,100 feet (640 m) per second, almost twice the speed of sound.[2]

Together, the Haags tested three popular questions. First, could Oswald have gotten off three shots with the Carcano? After the shot that missed, Kennedy's shooter would have had several seconds to fire two more shots. That would be several seconds to chamber a new round, aim, shoot, chamber another round, aim, and shoot again. "It is absolutely something that is realistically possible," Michael Haag told Ira Flatow, the host of National Public Radio's *Science Friday*.[1] Haag had done so several times on the range.

The second question the Haags addressed was whether a single bullet could have injured both Kennedy and Connally. The bullet recovered from Connally's stretcher in the hospital is often described as undamaged. Conspiracy theorists believe that a bullet that injured two men would be seriously misshapen. Again, the Haags tested this by firing a Carcano rifle loaded with the same kind of ammunition Oswald used.

Michael Haag fired the rifle at pine boards stacked to a depth of several feet and clamped upright. His father then separated the boards to reach the spent bullet. The bullet passed through 36 inches (91 cm) of boards without compressing, deforming, or fragmenting.[3] It could have caused multiple injuries in two people, but the Haags needed to perform another test to see if the injuries would be consistent with how the bullet had reportedly hurt both Kennedy and Connally.

In this test, they fired the gun at a target made of ballistic gel, which simulates human muscle. A short distance behind the gel was a witness panel. After the bullet passed through the gel, it then passed through the panel, leaving a bullet-shaped hole in the panel. The hole showed that the bullet had struck in profile, side first, because it was tumbling end over end, or yawing. "Time after time, the instant this bullet is back out into the atmosphere, it goes into yaw. From a science standpoint, it's repeatable," said Luke Haag.[4] A yawing bullet often hits on its side and does more damage than a bullet that is not yawing. It would cause the type of wide wound that doctors found on Connally.

Additional proof that the bullet that hit Connally was yawing can be found by studying photos of the bullet found on Connally's stretcher. When photographed from the side, the bullet appears undamaged. But when photographed from the rear, the bullet looks slightly misshapen. "This is the consequence of slamming into Governor Connally while in yaw. That squeezes the bullet just like you'd squeeze a toothpaste tube," said Luke Haag.[5] The Carcano bullet would have caused the injuries found on both men, and it would have been damaged just like the bullet found on Connally's stretcher.

Ballistics experts work in government crime labs and private consulting businesses that analyze evidence from crime scenes.

There was one more question the Haags wanted to answer. Could a single type of bullet have caused the wounds in Kennedy and Connally and then the fatal head shot? Many people believe it could not, which is why they think there must have been more than one shooter. To test this, the Haags mocked up a skull by placing a layer of flat animal bone over ballistic gel. When bullets passed through the bone, they did one of two things. Some yawed, which increased their level of damage. Others fragmented, which also made them more damaging. When Kennedy was shot in his head, the bullet fragmented, causing a larger wound. "[This] is the reason why the head shot looks so dramatically different and is so much more catastrophic," said Michael Haag.[6]

A shot from behind could have caused Kennedy's head to whip back as is seen in the Zapruder film. Larry Sturdivan is an expert in wound ballistics. When a bullet enters the brain, the brain absorbs the energy of the shot. "The tissue inside the skull was being moved around. It caused a massive amount of nerve stimulation to go down his spine. Every nerve in his body was stimulated. Now, since the back muscles are stronger than the abdominal muscles, that meant that Kennedy arched dramatically backwards," says Sturdivan.[7] Research by the Haags and Sturdivan confirmed that Oswald shot Kennedy from the Texas School Book Depository.

REMEMBERING WHEN JFK WAS SHOT

Nearly everyone who was alive when President John F. Kennedy was shot remembers the moment they heard about it. This includes the researchers and scientists who went on to study the assassination years later. "I was with my future wife, coming out of a music class," said firearms expert Luke Haag, who reexamined the assassination case in 2013.[8]

People remember this moment because so much hope had been placed in the popular President Kennedy, even among international leaders. Following the assassination, nearly 250,000 German people squeezed into West Berlin's John F. Kennedy Square to mourn his death. West Berlin mayor Willy Brandt said in a speech, "A flame went out for all those who had hoped for a just peace and a better life."[9]

As the so-called "grassy knoll" conspiracy theory is well known, many tourists visit the hill in Dealey Plaza. However, experts have concluded that Kennedy was shot from the Texas School Book Depository, not from the knoll.

Laser Mapping

Another conspiracy theory states that there was a shooter on a nearby grassy knoll. To find out if that was possible, Tony Grissim, an expert in examining firearms and gunshot evidence,

worked with Michael Haag to create a three-dimensional laser scan of Dealey Plaza. The pair set the scanning system up at several points around the plaza and on the sixth floor of the Depository. The system used mirrors and lasers to rapidly measure angles and distances in all directions around the setup. Once the measurements were made, a computer took several weeks to process all of the information to create a three-dimensional map of Dealey Plaza. The map included all roads, buildings, doorways, windows, and streetlamps, accurate to within an eighth of an inch (3 mm).

This map allows exact measurements to be made. From the grassy knoll, a shot to Kennedy would have been about 105 feet (32 m) at a four-degree downward angle.[10] This is well within the capability of a common rifle and of the Carcano.

But Michael Haag doesn't think the shot that killed Kennedy came from the grassy knoll. To shoot Kennedy from that spot may have been possible, and the shooter would have been hidden from the Secret Service behind a wooden fence. But

3-D LASER IMAGING

When a three-dimensional laser scan is made of an area, such as a plaza or a parking garage, it takes every measurement that is a straight line from the origin of the laser. Before three-dimensional laser scanning was available, a person had to take measurements with a tape measure or a measuring wheel. A measuring wheel is held against the ground as a technician walks a long distance, such as the width of a parking area. As the wheel turns, a calibrated counter totals the distance walked. When technicians got back to the office, they would sometimes realize that they had forgotten to measure the height of a step, the distance from one side of the street to the other, or something else. Three-dimensional laser scanning is more efficient because it helps eliminate having to make a second trip because of a forgotten measurement.

the person's back would have been fully exposed, a vulnerable position. "You're standing with your back to a parking lot," said Haag.[11] At any time, someone could have walked up behind a grassy knoll shooter, who would be focused on what was happening in the plaza. Haag has one more reason to discredit the grassy knoll theory. "There's not a bit of physical evidence," Haag said.[12]

Sound Studies

Witnesses interviewed by the House Select Committee were split on the question of where Kennedy's shooter was located. Some of the witnesses said the shots came from the Book Depository. Others said the shots came from the grassy knoll in the opposite direction. They also disagreed on the number of shots fired.

Professor Michael Hargather of the New Mexico Institute of Mining and Technology studies shock waves caused by explosions. "It's a major problem for our soldiers in Iraq and Afghanistan, to be able to understand where shooters are in these urban environments. Multiple buildings, multiple locations that the shock waves reverberate off of, can give us multiple sound signatures," Hargather says.[13]

In 2013, to address questions about the Kennedy assassination, Hargather studied a Carcano firing using a shadowgraph, which is a type of photo that can show sound

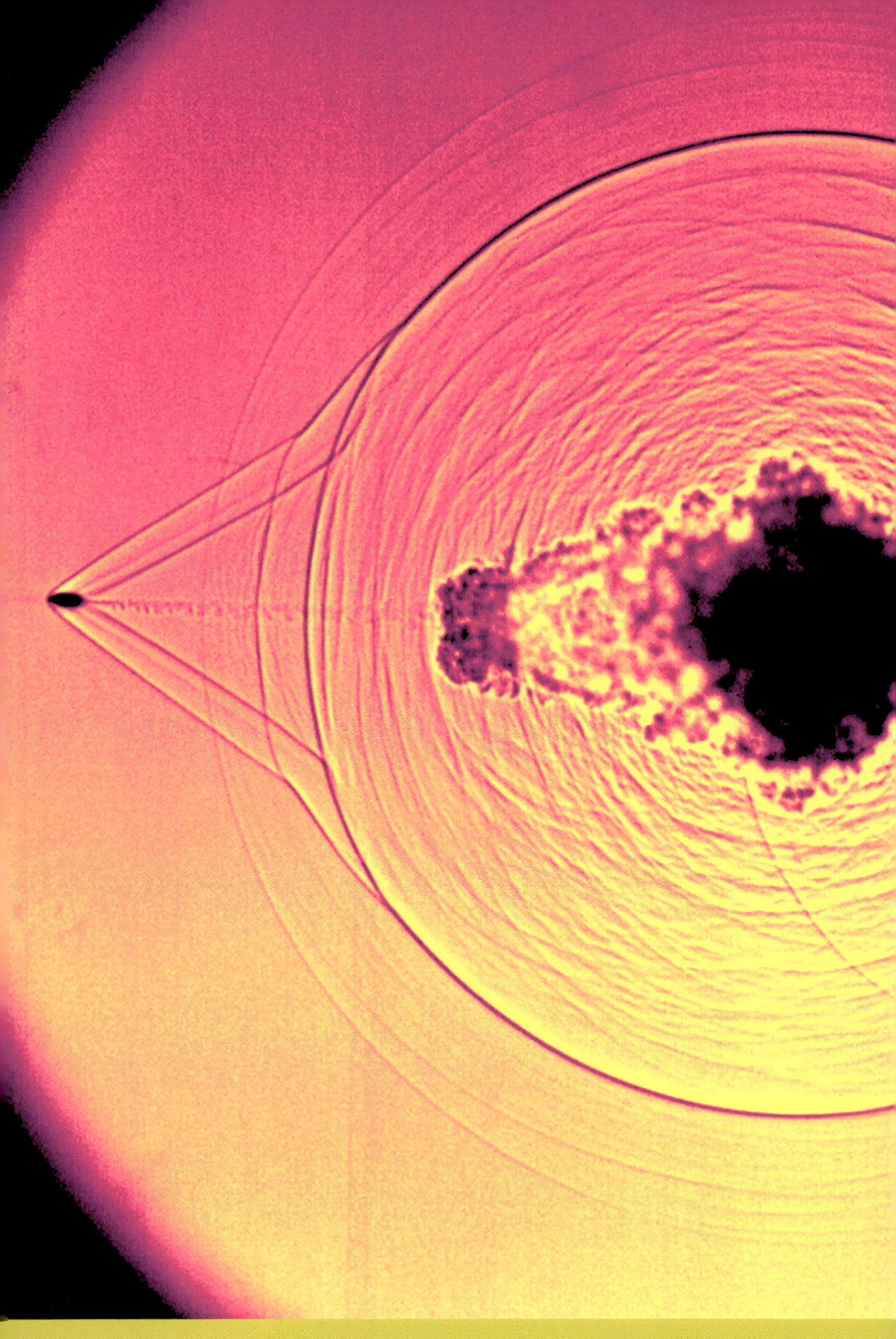

An example of a shadowgraph image showing the sound waves from a bullet being shot

PHOTOGRAPHING SOUND WITH SHADOWGRAPHS

As loud sounds pass through the air, they literally compress the gases, which then makes them denser than the surrounding air. It is this change in density that scientists photograph when they take a shadowgraph. All that is needed to take this type of photograph is a high-speed camera, a bright light beam, a reflective background, and of course, something to generate the loud bang, boom, or crack. When the photo is taken, the airwaves are captured as grey lines, sometimes shimmery but other times bold and distinct, depending on the sound.

waves. The shadowgraph revealed that when a Carcano fires, there are two sound waves. The bullet is supersonic, firing faster than the speed of sound. One sound wave, V-shaped, is from the bullet, and the second wave is from the gases that propel it forward. For each shot fired from the Carcano, witnesses would have heard two cracks, each ricocheting around the plaza. Based on the sounds, it would be almost impossible for a witness to tell the number of shots or where they originated. But all physical evidence points toward the conclusion that the shooter was at the sixth floor of the Depository.

CHAPTER EIGHT

CONTROVERSIES AND COVER-UPS

Both the Warren Commission and the House Select Committee ultimately agreed that Lee Harvey Oswald assassinated President John F. Kennedy. Both determined that he fired at Kennedy from the sixth floor of the Texas School Book Depository. Despite the fact that both investigations agreed on these key points and that much of the evidence, interviews, and conclusions are publicly available, conspiracy theories persist.

"The Kennedy assassination is a lot like a Rorschach test," said G. Robert Blakey, the chief counsel for the House Select Committee. "Give me a statement about the assassination; it really tells me more about you than it does about what happened."[1] People who were paranoid about Communists would expect to find a tie to the Soviet Union or Cuba. Those who didn't trust the government blamed the CIA and the FBI.

A Dallas street vendor sells a magazine-style conspiracy theory publication.

Thunder
ON THE MOUNTAIN
JFK
THE CASE FOR
CONSPIRACY
HIGH
TREASON
THE ASSASSINATION
OF PRESIDENT JOHN F. KENNEDY
WHAT REALLY HAPPENED
THE KILLING
OF A
PRESIDENT
ROBERT J. GRODEN

RORSCHACH TEST

The Rorschach test is also known as the inkblot test. The person who is taking the test is asked to look at a black inkblot and tell the tester what they see. This is the second-most commonly used forensic test and is believed to reveal information about the test-taker's personality and emotions. Some people believe the same is true with the Kennedy assassination. A person who doesn't trust the government is likely to believe that the government is covering up facts about Kennedy's death. Someone who focuses on international intrigue may suspect the Soviets. Someone who gets their information from science will stick with the facts.

For some people, it is easy to continue to believe that one of the conspiracy theories may be true. Broken chains of evidence sow doubt. Facts incorrectly stated and later corrected might point to a cover-up.

Luke Haag has his own idea about why people latch onto conspiracy theories:

> *There's something in our psyche that likes a mystery, that likes to think there's got to be more to it than just some loner, loser, ne'er-do-well Marxist or whatever the person's philosophy might be, could kill the leader of a country. . . . My urging would be for those who have a scientific mind to find out what the physical evidence is, then to understand that physical evidence.*[2]

Documents Opened

Conspiracy theorists may be fueled by the fact that years after the Kennedy assassination, some government files on the

YEARS OF CONSPIRACY THEORIES

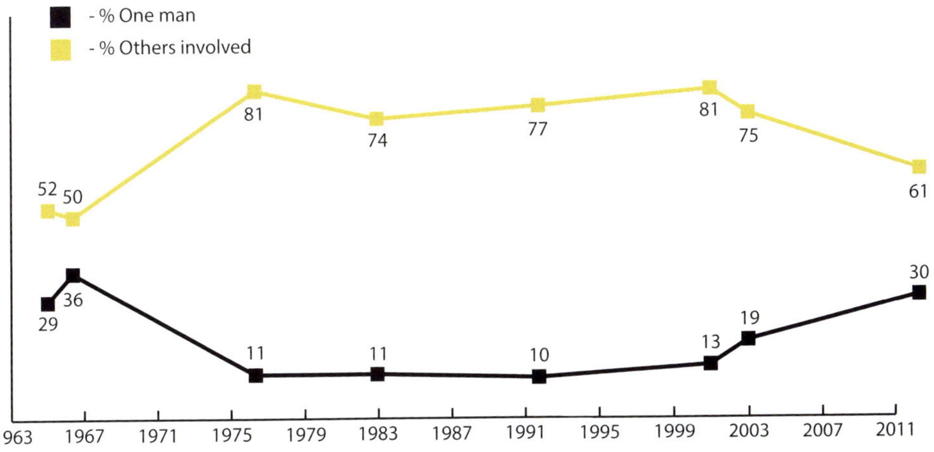

Decades after John F. Kennedy was killed, people continue to believe conspiracy theories about the assassination. Between 1963 and 2011, the majority of Americans polled by Gallup believed that there was more than one shooter, despite the fact that many experts have pinned the crime on Lee Harvey Oswald alone.[3]

On April 26, 2018, the National Archives uploaded 18,731 previously unseen documents related to the Kennedy assassination to its website.[5]

case have still not been released to the public. In October 2017, the last of the closed files were supposed to be released, but President Donald Trump gave the agencies that held the files time to review them. The documents were studied, and on April 26, 2018, most were uploaded to the National Archives website. Still, some of these public versions of the documents were heavily redacted, meaning that blocks of text were blacked out and kept secret. This was done because of "identifiable national security, law enforcement, and foreign affairs concerns," according to a memorandum issued by President Trump.[4] Many of these documents come from the FBI and CIA.

Among the material released by the National Archives was testimony given in 1978 to the House Select Committee on Assassinations by then CIA Mexico City station chief David Atlee Phillips. Phillips was questioned about the possibility that Oswald might have worked with or for a foreign power, specifically the Soviets or the Cubans. "I would like for it to come out that [Cuba's leader] Fidel Castro was responsible or that the Soviets were responsible," Phillips said. "But I know of no evidence to show that the Cubans or the Soviets put him up to it, and I just have to go along on the side that he was kind of a loony fellow who decided to shoot the president, and he did."[6]

When the remaining files are finally opened, new information may be discovered. As of 2019, this reveal was scheduled for October 26, 2021. This new information may support one of the conspiracy theories. It may answer a previously unanswered question. But until new information comes to light, people can only continue to look at the publicly available information in new ways. One element of the case that still stirs persistent questions is Oswald's motive. Why did Oswald shoot Kennedy?

Why Did Oswald Do It?

Stephen Diamond is a forensic psychologist. In addition to trying to figure out how to prevent people from committing crimes, forensic psychologists look at the kinds of people who commit certain crimes and study what motivates them to act. Diamond has tried to figure out Oswald's motive.

Diamond believes some clues can be found in Oswald's early life. Oswald's father died while his mother was pregnant, leaving her struggling to support Oswald and his two brothers. Because she worked, other people took care of Oswald, and there was evidence that he was physically abused by at least one babysitter. While the family lived in the Bronx in New York

A family photo shows young Oswald on a trip to the Bronx Zoo in New York City, where he grew up.

City, Oswald was sent to a juvenile reformatory for skipping school. While in this facility, a psychiatric evaluation of Oswald stated that he had "a vivid fantasy life, turning around the topics of omnipotence and power, through which he tries to compensate for his present shortcomings and frustrations."[7] During his early teens, Oswald also hit his mother several times and even pulled a knife on his sister-in-law during a disagreement.

According to Diamond, these behaviors show that Oswald had problems with impulse control, especially when he was angry. He also believes that Oswald would today be diagnosed with oppositional defiant disorder or conduct disorder. Children and teens with oppositional defiant disorder are generally unruly, pick arguments, and have problems with anyone who has authority over them. They are extremely negative and hostile and often act out toward teachers, parents, and other authority figures. Sometimes they try to get revenge. Conduct disorder is more severe than oppositional defiant disorder, and symptoms usually appear by the time the person is 16 years old. People who have this disorder have no empathy for others, especially the people they bully. Diamond believes that people like Oswald who commit murder may have these identifiable disorders, but two things drive them to kill—anger and a desire for attention.

Oswald may not have worked in league with a foreign power, but he had been to Mexico City just three weeks prior to the assassination. Oswald wanted to travel to Cuba but was denied a travel visa. There is speculation that he may have decided to assassinate Kennedy in an attempt to impress Fidel Castro, Cuba's Communist leader, and gain admission to Cuba. Oswald's admiration of and fascination with Communism put him at odds with Kennedy's philosophies and, in the context of the Cold War, may have turned him against the United States in general.

Conspiracy Theories Continue

Despite all that is known, conspiracy theories persist. Was Louie David Witt really the Umbrella Man? Some people wonder if the Umbrella Man was a Soviet sympathizer. They also wonder about a mysterious woman known as the Babushka Lady. She can be seen in the Zapruder film wearing a babushka headscarf, traditionally worn by Russian women. No government agency has ever been able to identify her.

Perhaps the most believable conspiracy, for those who know history, is that Castro or someone who was pro-Cuba was behind Kennedy's death. Kennedy's assassination occurred at the height of the Cold War. Shortly after Kennedy took office on January 20, 1961, the CIA launched an invasion of Cuba. The Bay of Pigs invasion involved 1,400 US-trained Cuban fighters who had fled their Cuban homeland when the Communists took over under Castro. The invasion was a complete failure, with 114 fighters killed and 1,100 captured.[8]

Later, in 1962, Kennedy and Soviet Union leader Nikita Khrushchev engaged in a tense 13-day military standoff over Soviet cruise missiles being assembled in Cuba. Only 90 miles (145 km) from the United States, these nuclear-enabled missiles were capable of reaching targets on the US East Coast, such as Washington, DC. Kennedy sent the US Navy to block the Soviets' path to Cuba. No more missiles could make it to the island, but the Soviets might have seen this as an act of war. This Cuban Missile Crisis lasted for 13 days as Americans waited for a nuclear war to start. Eventually, Khrushchev and the Soviet Union agreed to remove its missiles from Cuba. The

THE BABUSHKA LADY

With multiple government investigations and calls for information, home movies and photographs have been collected from people who lined the motorcade route on the day Kennedy was assassinated. But one person has never come forward with her photographs. The Zapruder film shows the Babushka Lady, a woman wearing a light-colored coat and headscarf. In the film, she can be seen holding a camera in front of her face. She was standing close to the limousine when the shots were fired. She is noticeable in the film because as other people ducked or ran away, she remained in place, seeming to focus on Kennedy's car. In 1970, Beverly Oliver claimed to be the Babushka Lady, but Oliver was 17 years old and slender in 1963. The woman in the photos was much older. Who she was remains a mystery.

ANOTHER THEORY: UFOs?

UFO enthusiast Timothy Hunter claimed that he was mailed a secret Kennedy document in 1999. Hunter said the document came from an unknown person who claimed to have worked for the CIA from 1960 to 1974 and rescued the document when numerous sensitive files were being burned. One scorched memo requested a review of all UFO documents within the CIA. Another, a letter, stated that "Lancer" had been asking questions that "we cannot allow."[9] Lancer was the CIA's codename for Kennedy. Because of these documents, some UFO believers think Kennedy was killed to keep him from uncovering what the CIA really knows about UFOs.

United States agreed not to invade Cuba and also to remove missiles from Turkey, near the border of the Soviet Union. Constant tension could have resulted in a Cuban plan to kill Kennedy. But so far, no information to support this theory has been made public.

Although the Kennedy assassination happened more than 50 years ago, Nicholas Nalli believes it is important to investigate cases like this that remain surrounded by controversy and conspiracy theories. Nalli is a senior research scientist at I.M. Systems Group, Inc., a company that works with environmental data for clients around the world. In April 2018, he authored a study about the Kennedy assassination. Nalli used force calculations and data on the transfer of momentum and energy. He was able to show that Kennedy's motions in the film were consistent with a rear shot from a Carcano rifle at the distance of the Depository.

Kennedy is remembered by numerous memorials, including the John F. Kennedy Center for the Performing Arts in Washington, DC.

Nalli undertook this work because he had been interested in the Kennedy assassination since he was a child. His study may not prove that Oswald acted alone, but it does prove that the fatal shot came from the Depository and not the grassy knoll. Nalli believes his work shows how relevant today's science is to yesterday's mysteries.

He also believes it is vital to teach young thinkers how to evaluate information. "Given the current trendiness of news that [is] not based on facts, the study shows that thorough scientific investigation can make a difference in supporting one theory over another," Nalli says.[10] Maybe someday, new investigative techniques or newfound evidence can definitively close the case of President Kennedy's assassination.

TIMELINE

1959

- Lee Harvey Oswald defects from the United States to the Soviet Union.

1961

- On January 20, John F. Kennedy is sworn in as the thirty-fifth president of the United States.

1962

- On June 1, Oswald and his wife, Marina, return to the United States.

1963

- On April 10, Oswald attempts to shoot Major General Edwin A. Walker.
- In September, Oswald travels to Mexico City to visit the Cuban and Soviet embassies.
- On November 22, at approximately 12:30 p.m. local time, President Kennedy is shot during a visit to Dallas, Texas.
- On November 22, at approximately 1:00 p.m., President Kennedy is declared dead.
- On November 22, at approximately 1:50 p.m., Oswald is arrested.
- On November 22, at approximately 2:38 p.m., Johnson is sworn in as president.
- On November 24, Oswald is shot to death by Jack Ruby.
- On November 29, *Life* magazine publishes images from the Zapruder film, showing Kennedy being assassinated.
- On November 29, President Lyndon B. Johnson creates the Warren Commission to investigate the assassination.

1964

- In March, Ruby is convicted of Oswald's killing.

1968

- On April 4, civil rights leader Martin Luther King Jr. is shot and killed in a US political assassination less than five years after Kennedy's death.

1975

- On March 6, Geraldo Rivera shows the full Zapruder film on *Good Night America*.

1976

- In September, the House of Representatives Select Committee on Assassinations is created to investigate the assassinations of Kennedy and King.

2018

- On April 26, the National Archives uploads thousands of previously unseen documents related to the Kennedy assassination onto its website to be viewed publicly.

ESSENTIAL FACTS

SIGNIFICANT EVENTS

- On November 22, 1963, President John F. Kennedy was shot to death while on his way to deliver a speech in Dallas, Texas. Later that same day, Dallas police arrested Lee Harvey Oswald for the assassination. Oswald, who was later killed by a bystander as police moved him between jails, never admitted to shooting Kennedy.

- After Kennedy's death, the FBI and numerous other government agencies investigated the assassination. Kennedy's successor, President Lyndon B. Johnson, formed a commission to investigate. A second government committee also investigated the assassination in 1976.

- For years following Kennedy's death, questions and theories about how he died have persisted. The federal government's investigations have all pointed to Oswald as Kennedy's sole killer. But many people continue to believe there was a conspiracy.

KEY PLAYERS

- President John F. Kennedy was assassinated in 1963 as he was preparing to run for a second term as president.

- Lee Harvey Oswald was a Communist sympathizer who was arrested on suspicion of killing Kennedy.

- Abraham Zapruder, a Dallas business owner, captured a home movie of Kennedy being shot. As the most complete film of the assassination, the Zapruder film was used in multiple investigations.

- Jack Ruby shot and killed Oswald, saying he was angry about Kennedy's assassination.

- Lyndon B. Johnson became president when Kennedy died and organized a commission to investigate Kennedy's death.

- US Supreme Court justice Earl Warren chaired the presidential commission that investigated the assassination. He was a friend to the Kennedy family.

IMPACT ON SOCIETY

The assassination of President John F. Kennedy threw the United States into a period of mourning and speculation about who was responsible. Evidence points to Lee Harvey Oswald as the man who shot Kennedy. But many people have theorized that there is more to it. Because the assassination itself came at the height of the Cold War, investigators looked into the possibility that the Soviet Union was involved. Conspiracy theories touched on organized crime and even US government agencies themselves. The president's assassination also resulted in efforts to prevent more political assassinations from occurring in the United States, and it left a lasting impact on Americans who will always remember the day their president was shot.

QUOTE

"There's something in our psyche that likes a mystery, that likes to think there's got to be more to it . . . [for someone to] kill the leader of a country. . . . My urging would be for those who have a scientific mind to find out what the physical evidence is, then to understand that physical evidence."

—*Luke Haag, firearms expert who investigated the Kennedy assassination in 2013*

GLOSSARY

accomplice
Someone who helps accomplish a task. Often used to describe someone who has helped commit a crime.

ballistics
The science of projectiles and firearms.

bootleg
Illegally produced and sold.

casing
In ammunition, the sleeve that contains the gunpowder and bullet.

Communist
Someone who holds the political belief that property should be owned by the group with members working as they are able and being paid what they need. During the Cold War, members of the Communist Party USA were hostile to American capitalism and supported the Soviet Union.

conspiracy
A secret plan to do something harmful or illegal.

defect
To leave one's home country to live in another, often in pursuit of a national ideology different than that of one's home country.

embassy
The official place in a foreign country where an ambassador works to represent his or her country.

forensic
Characterized by the use of scientific techniques to investigate a crime.

motorcade
A procession of motor vehicles, often escorting a prominent individual.

pathology
The science of disease causes and effects, especially the examination of tissue samples in the laboratory.

Soviet Union
A former Communist country in Europe and Asia composed of 15 Communist republics under a single Communist leadership.

tracheotomy
The medical procedure that allows making a hole in a patient's windpipe, through the throat, to help the person breathe.

visa
An official authorization permitting entry into and travel within a country.

ADDITIONAL RESOURCES

SELECTED BIBLIOGRAPHY

"The House Select Committee on Assassinations Report." *National Archives: The President John F. Kennedy Assassination Records Collection*, 1979, archives.gov. Accessed 25 Apr. 2019.

"The Warren Commission Report." *National Archives: The President John F. Kennedy Assassination Records Collection*, 1964, archives.gov. Accessed 25 Apr. 2019.

FURTHER READINGS

Burling, Alexis. *The Kennedys*. Abdo, 2016.

Sarmiento, Kimberly. *The Story of John F. Kennedy 100 Years after His Birth*. Atlantic Publishing, 2016.

Swanson, James L. *"The President Has Been Shot!" The Assassination of John F. Kennedy*. Scholastic, 2013.

ONLINE RESOURCES

To learn more about the assassination of John F. Kennedy, please visit **abdobooklinks.com** or scan this QR code. These links are routinely monitored and updated to provide the most current information available.

MORE INFORMATION

For more information on this subject, contact or visit the following organizations:

JOHN F. KENNEDY PRESIDENTIAL LIBRARY AND MUSEUM

Columbia Point, Boston, MA 02125

617-514-1600

jfklibrary.org

The library and museum are part of a park that overlooks the ocean. Tour the museum to learn about Kennedy's life, leadership, and political legacy.

THE SIXTH FLOOR MUSEUM

411 Elm St., Dallas, TX 75202

214-747-6660

jfk.org

Exhibits at this museum explore the life and assassination of Kennedy, and their impact on society. Researchers can make appointments to explore the books, oral history recordings, and other media housed in the Reading Room.

SOURCE NOTES

CHAPTER 1. THE ASSASSINATION

1. Sophail Al-Jamea, Darla Cameron, Todd Lindeman, and Gene Thorp. "A Moment That Changed Everything." *Washington Post*, 16 Nov. 2013, washingtonpost.com. Accessed 23 July 2019.

2. John Mancini. "JFK's Final Hour, in the Words of His Widow and Other Eyewitnesses." *Quartz*, 22 Nov. 2018, qz.com. Accessed 23 July 2019.

3. Rick Hampson. "JFK: The Moments before the Moment Everything Changed." *USA Today*, 18 Nov. 2013, usatoday.com. Accessed 23 July 2019.

4. CBS Sunday Morning. "JFK Assassination: Cronkite Informs a Shocked Nation." *YouTube*, 17 Nov. 2013, youtube.com. Accessed 23 July 2019.

5. Public Radio International. "American Experience: International Reaction to the Death of JFK." *YouTube*, 22 Nov. 2013, youtube.com. Accessed 13 Feb. 2019.

CHAPTER 2. THE SHOOTER

1. "Chapter 3: The Shots from the Texas School Book Depository." *The Warren Report*. Washington DC: The US Government Printing Office, 1964, archives.gov. 65. Accessed 16 Feb. 2019.

2. "Chapter 4: The Assassin." *The Warren Report*. Washington, DC: US Government Printing Office, 1964, archives.gov. 180. Accessed 23 July 2019.

3. "Chapter 4: The Assassin."

4. William Cran and Ben Loeterman. "Who Was Lee Harvey Oswald?" *Frontline*, 19 Nov. 2013, pbs.org. Accessed 27 Feb. 2019.

5. Cran and Loeterman, "Who Was Lee Harvey Oswald?"

6. "Chapter 4: The Assassin."

7. HelmerReenburg. "April 11, 1963 - General Edwin Walker Interviewed after Assassination Attempt." *YouTube*, 24 Dec. 2012, youtube.com. Accessed 23 July 2019.

8. "Chapter 7: Lee Harvey Oswald: Background and Possible Motives." *The Warren Report*. Washington, DC: US Government Printing Office, 1964, archives.gov. 377. Accessed 23 July 2019.

CHAPTER 3. GATHERING EVIDENCE

1. Aaron Foly. "Why JFK's Limousine Stayed in Service for 13 Years after Dallas." *Jalopnik*, 22 Nov. 2013, jalopnik.com. Accessed 23 July 2019.

2. Christopher Wynn. "Missing Radio Tapes, An Alleged Cleanup: JFK Limousine Part of Assassination Conspiracy Lore." *Dallas Morning News*, May 2013, dallasnews.com. Accessed 22 Apr. 2019.

CHAPTER 4. THE WARREN COMMISSION

1. Evan Andrews. "9 Things You May Not Know about the Warren Commission." *History*, 18 Nov. 2013, history.com. Accessed 23 July 2019.

2. "Warren Commission – Introduction." *National Archives: The President John F. Kennedy Assassination Records Collection*, 1964, archives.gov. Accessed 20 Feb. 2019.

3. *Report on President's Commission on the Assassination of President John F. Kennedy.* Washington, DC: US Government Printing Office, 1964, govinfo.gov. 1. Accessed 23 July 2019.

4. Steven M. Gillon. "Why the Public Stopped Believing the Government about JFK's Murder." *History*, 30 Oct. 2017, history.com. Accessed 23 July 2019.

5. *Report on President's Commission on the Assassination of President John F. Kennedy.*

6. Art Swift. "Majority in U.S. Still Believe JFK Killed in a Conspiracy." *Gallup*, 15 Nov. 2013, gallup.com. Accessed 23 July 2019.

CHAPTER 5. THE ZAPRUDER FILM

1. Steve Rose. "Abraham Zapruder: The Man behind History's Most Infamous Home Movie." *Guardian*, 14 Nov. 2013, theguardian.com. Accessed 23 July 2019.

2. Michael Granberry. "How Did Abraham Zapruder's Film of JFK's Assassination Alter a Family? Learn from his Granddaughter at SMU." *Dallas Morning News*, 16 Nov. 2016, dallasnews.com. Accessed 1 Mar. 2019.

3. Granberry, "How Did Abraham Zapruder's Film of JFK's Assassination Alter a Family? Learn from his Granddaughter at SMU."

4. Abraham Zapruder. "JFK Assassination, Frame 313." *Time*, 1963, time.com. Accessed 23 July 2019.

5. Glenn Garvin. "The $16 Million Film of the JFK Assassination That Carried a Curse." *Miami Herald*, 29 Nov. 2017, miamiherald.com. Accessed 1 March 2019.

6. "Geraldo Rivera: 'Well Past Time' to Release Everything on JFK Assassination." *FOX Insider*, 21 Oct. 2017, foxnews.com. Accessed 20 Feb. 2019.

SOURCE NOTES CONTINUED

CHAPTER 6. A COMMITTEE ON ASSASSINATIONS

1. "The House Select Committee on Assassinations Report." *National Archives: The President John F. Kennedy Assassination Records Collection*, 1979, archives.gov. Accessed 23 July 2019.

2. "House Panel Issues Subpoenas in Inquiry on 2 Assassinations." *New York Times*, 18 Nov. 1976, nytimes.com. Accessed 20 Aug. 2019.

3. History.com editors. "Martin Luther King, Jr." *History*, 9 Nov. 2009, history.com. Accessed 23 July 2019.

CHAPTER 7. FIFTY YEARS LATER

1. Science Friday. "Using Ballistic Basics to Crack 'Cold Case JFK.' " *National Public Radio*, 22 Nov. 2013, npr.org. Accessed 3 Mar. 2019.

2. "Cold Case JFK." *NOVA*, season 40, episode 2, *PBS*, 13 Nov. 2013, pbs.org. Accessed 20 Aug. 2019.

3. "Cold Case JFK."

4. "Cold Case JFK."

5. "Using Ballistic Basics to Crack 'Cold Case JFK.' "

6. "Using Ballistic Basics to Crack 'Cold Case JFK.' "

7. "Cold Case JFK."

8. "Cold Case JFK."

9. Vincent Bugliosi. *Reclaiming History: The Assassination of President John F. Kennedy*. Norton, 2007. 156.

10. "Cold Case JFK."

11. "Using Ballistic Basics to Crack 'Cold Case JFK.' "

12. "Using Ballistic Basics to Crack 'Cold Case JFK.' "

13. "Cold Case JFK."

CHAPTER 8. CONTROVERSIES AND COVER-UPS

1. "Cold Case JFK." *NOVA*, season 40, episode 2, *PBS*, 13 Nov. 2013, pbs.org. Accessed 20 Aug. 2019.

2. Science Friday. "Using Ballistic Basics to Crack 'Cold Case JFK.'" *National Public Radio*, 22 Nov. 2013, npr.org. Accessed 3 Mar. 2019.

3. Art Swift. "Majority in U.S. Still Believe JFK Killed in a Conspiracy." *Gallup*, 15 Nov. 2013, gallup.com. Accessed 23 July 2019.

4. Todd Gillman. "Trump Keeps Some JFK Documents Sealed until 2021 as Archives Release Final Batch." *Dallas Morning News*, 26 Apr. 26 2018, dallasnews.com. Accessed Mar. 4, 2019.

5. Chris Morris. "New JFK Assassination Records Made Public, but Trump Seals Others for Another 3.5 Years." *Fortune*, 26 Apr. 2018, fortune.com. Accessed 4 Mar. 2019.

6. "Trump Keeps Some JFK Documents Sealed until 2021 as Archives Release Final Batch."

7. Stephen A. Diamond. "Why Did Lee Harvey Oswald Kill John Fitzgerald Kennedy?" *Psychology Today*, 21 Nov. 2013, psychologytoday.com. Accessed 22 Feb. 2019.

8. History.com editors. "Bay of Pigs Invasion." *History*, 27 Oct. 2009, history.com. Accessed Mar. 4, 2019.

9. Natalie Wolchover. "CIA Cover-up Alleged in JFK's 'Secret UFO Inquiry.'" *Livescience*, 20 Apr. 2014, livescience.com. Accessed 23 July 2019.

10. Nicholas R. Nalli. "Gunshot-Wound Dynamics Model for John F. Kennedy Assassination." *Heliyon*, 30 Apr. 2018, heliyon.com. Accessed 4 Mar. 2019.

INDEX

ABOUT THE AUTHOR

Sue Bradford Edwards grew up hearing about President Kennedy's assassination. Her father worked at a television station in Lubbock, Texas, and was at work when the shooting occurred. She is the author or coauthor of 16 other titles from Abdo Publishing, including *Hidden Human Computers, The Dakota Access Pipeline,* and *Black Lives Matter.*